# THE HERALD
## DIARY

# THE HERALD DIARY

## In Purrsuit of Happiness

## Ken Smith

BLACK & WHITE PUBLISHING

First published 2010
by Black & White Publishing Ltd
29 Ocean Drive, Edinburgh EH6 6JL


1 3 5 7 9 10 8 6 4 2   10 11 12 13


ISBN: 978 1 84502 315 7

A CIP catalogue record for this book is available from the British Library.


Typeset by Ellipsis Books Limited, Glasgow
Printed and bound by MPG Books Ltd, Bodmin

# Contents

# Introduction

You've got to laugh if you come from Scotland. Fortunately, the readers of *The Herald*, when they hear a funny tale or see a funny picture, take the time to send it to the newspaper's Diary column, which, thanks to the Internet, is now read all over the world.

Even in these times of job losses, roller-coaster house prices, changing governments, and greedy bankers, people are still smiling, still cracking jokes, and still seeing the funny side of life.

These are the stories that have kept the readers of the Diary amused in recent times, and we are sure they will bring a smile to even the most grim-faced banker, politician or traffic warden.

Enjoy.

# Introduction

# 1
# We'll Drink to That

Bossed about by idiots at work, and with mounting chores at home, many a Scot seeks solace in the pub. Overindulging is of course a curse on the country, but for those who don't, the pub is still the one place to tell bad jokes, air outrageous theories, and hear the tallest of tales. Here are a few of them.

"A REAL woman is a man's best friend," declared the chap in the pub. "She'll reassure him when he feels insecure, comfort him after a bad day, and inspire him to do things he never thought he could do. She'll help him express his emotions, give in to his most intimate desires, and always make him feel like the most confident, sexy man in the room.

"No, wait – I'm getting mixed up with alcohol."

CHARLIE ANDREWS in Greenock heard a chap in the pub tell his pals that going home drunk the previous night had been one of his worst nights ever. When they asked why, he told them: "I stood at the bottom of the stairs, drunk. So I decided to take off my clothes and shoes and tiptoe upstairs."

That didn't sound so bad, said his pals, until he added: "Then I realised I was still on the bus."

READER Iain Carmichael was in Chaplin's Hotel in Bellshill, one of the first Lanarkshire hostelries showing football in 3D, which is the latest technology toy from Sky.

Says Iain: "There was a fair crowd all wearing the standard issue Roy Orbison type 3D glasses enjoying the game, when in walked an elderly local, who, perhaps not up to speed with the new TV technology, exclaimed: "Bloody Hell! I've never seen so many blin' folk all in the wan pub before."

"I SAW a magazine," said the chap in the pub, "which wanted readers to send in funny photographs of the stupidest things they have done while drunk." He then added: "So I sent them my wedding album."

"I DON'T like karaoke," declared the chap in the pub the other night. "If I wanted to hear a drunken, shrieking version of an Amy Winehouse song, I'd go to an Amy Winehouse concert."

DURING the office Christmas party season a reader overheard a gently swaying chap approach a colleague in a Glasgow bar and ask her out.

"No, sorry, I would be cheating," she replied.

"What? Have you got a boyfriend?" the chap persisted, before she delivered the killer line:

"No. I would be cheating myself."

YES, MEN can be so brave when they are in the pub. Like the chap we overheard who told his pals when discussing the great weather: "I was so hot in bed last night I had to cuddle up to the wife to get cold."

THE WARM weather in Glasgow brought out some very old shorts and t-shirts, but also even older jokes. That must be the reason why a reader in Clydebank phoned to tell us: "The flasher who drinks in our pub said he was thinking of retiring. But he decided in the end that he would stick it out for another year."

READER Tommy Burns from Portpatrick walked into a Newton Stewart pub – not the poshest, but a decent shop – and, seeing a chap drinking a brandy, it fair put him in mind for one. "Brandy, please," he asked the barmaid who stood there for an uncomfortable second or two before telling him: "We only have the one brandy glass."

A STUDENT attending one of Glasgow's nightclubs was in the queue when the steward bellowed at folk to stand back from the door. The mouthy girl at the front snapped back: "Want tae no shout in ma ear!" The steward merely replied: "Want tae no staun unner ma mooth."

"I SAW this cute young thing in the bar on Saturday night," said the pub loudmouth. "So I went up and asked her what her name was. 'Chantelle,' she said. So I told her, 'Come on, you can tell me.'"

"ON REFLECTION," said the chap in the pub the other night, "when my wife proudly said she could get into the same skirts from before she was married, I shouldn't have replied: 'I wish I could.'"

A READER swears he heard a local in a Port Glasgow pub telling his pal he had just watched a very good film starring "Sylvester . . . Whatsisname?" 'Stallone?' his mate replied: "Naw. It finished ages ago.'"

"THEY say," said the nineteenth-hole philosopher at an Ayrshire golf club, "that forty is the new thirty. But just try telling that to a traffic cop who's pulled you over."

WHEN Easter approached, a bar-room philosopher argued: "Let's be honest, if it wasn't for Easter eggs and Christmas presents, Christianity would be long gone by now."

A GLASGOW reader overheard a medical student tell her pal she'd had too much to drink, but her pal said she was fine and challenged her to ask her anything so she could prove it.

"OK. What does serotonin do?" asked the sober one. "Unfair!" replied the drinker. "I don't know who Sarah Tonin is."

THE CHAP in the pub declared: "My girlfriend asked what she could do to make her bum look smaller." He added: "I told her to move to America."

"WHENEVER I see a woman with a tattoo," said the loudmouth in the pub, "I think to myself, 'Here's a girl who's capable of making a decision she'll regret in the future.'"

WE FEEL the chap in the West-End bar was being a bit harsh the other night when he told a woman looking at her stars in a newspaper: "Yes, millions of planets and stars have spent billions of years lining themselves up just to let you know that you'll meet someone with nice eyes today."

A CHAP going into a bar in Edinburgh spotted two comely young women and heard one whisper to the other as he went past, "Nine."

Chuffed at the thought they were marking him out of ten, he was thus deflated when his mate he was meeting asked him: "Did you see those two German birds at the bar?"

WE ADMIRED the linguistic dexterity of a BBC employee in a West-End bar who was explaining to a chap who asked what she did for a living that she was a film editor. When he asked what that involved, she told him: "Well, to cut a long story short . . ."

CLEARLY someone unaware of the terrible suffering in Haiti was the loudmouth in the Glasgow bar who declared: "Did you see the chap they rescued who had survived for eleven days on Coke, beer and biscuits? I did that for three years at Glasgow Yoonie."

GOOD to see pubs holding Burns Nights, which means that folk don't have to be members of stuffy golf or rugby clubs in order to attend one. At the inaugural Burns Supper at the Velvet Elvis bar/diner in Partick, speaker Phil Strange explained: "Owner Alan Mawn told me not to worry about being witty or clever. 'Just be yourself,' he said."

A CHAP in the pub mournfully declared: "I'm so sad I even take wrong turnings in the car so the sat-nav will talk to me."

A STORY about Bunnahabhain whisky from Islay reminds a publican of when it was his malt of the month.

He tells us: "Standing behind the bar with my son, I asked him, as the better printer, to put the offer on the blackboard. 'Which one?' he asked. 'Bunnahabhain,' I replied. Wordlessly, he handed me the chalk back."

"DOES anyone else think," asked the chap in the bar the other day, "that microwave minutes last an awful lot longer than normal minutes?"

"SOME of life's great lessons," a reader heard a student spout to pals in a Byres Road pub, "can be learned from Samson."

Our reader hoped for some Old Testament erudition, but instead the student added: "Rule number one: Never trust a woman."

"SURELY with a name like Judas," said the philosopher in the golf club bar, "Jesus should have been a bit suspicious."

"PHONED a guy who had a car for sale in the paper," said the toper in the pub. "I asked him if it was an estate. And he said, 'No, it's in excellent condition.'"

A LANARKSHIRE reader realised the new barmaid in his local was perhaps new at the job when an old regular took his empty pint glass up to the bar and told her: "Another dead man."

The girl replied: "OK, a pint of Deadman," and started frantically looking at the names on the beer taps.

READER Tom Burnett tells us of being at a function where the speaker thanked the bar staff, Nick and Roger. As the guests added their thanks, the speaker added: "That's not their real names – it's just what they do all day."

WE ARE told about the Inverclyde golf club member who regaled the bar about his pal who spent the night drunkenly playing the one-armed bandit.

Going home late at night he couldn't open his door, and when a puzzled joiner later took off the lock he found it was jammed with coins, and the handle had obviously been overused.

"THE WIFE said she wanted to be pampered on Valentine's Day," said the loudmouth in the pub. "But I had a look at them in the super-market, and there's no way she would fit in them."

"I'D A TERRIBLE argument with the wife the other night," said the loudmouth in the pub. "And she became historical."

"Don't you mean hysterical?" replied his mate. "No. She kept on bringing up all the things I've done wrong over the past ten years."

"I DON'T think I'll win the lottery," said the chap in the pub. "There were two pens on the lottery stand at the newsagent, and I couldn't even pick the one that worked."

JOHN CALLAGHAN tells us that at his local golf club, the barmaid was told that the soup of the day was venison broth. She then chalked up on the menu board to the puzzlement of customers: "Venice and Broth."

"Deer, oh deer," says John.

# 2
# On the Buses

**Many people drive to work, cut off from their fellow man. But fortunately for the Diary, car ownership in Glasgow is well below the national average, meaning thousands still use buses, where overhearing the strangest of tales just cannot be helped.**

CALUM McPHEE on Glasgow's 66 bus saw a mother getting on in the West End with two girls in Glasgow Academy uniforms. When they sat down she enthusiastically informed them that she had treats for them. When they excitedly asked what, she replied that she had been to the deli in Byres Road and had tubs of marinated garlic, sun-dried tomatoes and olives.

At that, the chap sitting in front shook his head, turned round and offered each of the girls a Wagon Wheel.

"WHAT'S your pet hate?" asked the young girl of her friend on the bus into Glasgow the other day. "Having her squeaky toy hidden," she replied, perhaps misunderstanding the question.

JAMIE STEWART was on a bus in the West End's Byres Road when a rough-looking chap boarded and sat beside a rather posh elderly lady from Kelvinside in the seats reserved for the elderly and infirm.

Minutes later, the jaikie broke wind so loudly it could be heard by all the passengers.

"Don't worry, hen," he turned and told the shocked Kelvinside lady. "They'll probably think it was me."

The bus was in such an uproar the poor woman got off at the next stop.

A READER on the 66 bus into Glasgow overheard two young chaps who hadn't seen each other for a while. In their conversation, one informed the other that he was on the dole. When his pal asked what it was like, he replied: "Well, the money's not great, but the hours are fantastic."

BUS DRIVERS in the city are told not to stop for anyone who is not at a bus stop. But a reader tells us he was on a night bus in Glasgow when the driver, obviously feeling sorry for the chap on a cold night, stopped for a passenger gently swaying on the pavement who held out his hand in between stops. He wished he hadn't bothered when he opened the doors and the chap merely inquired: "Huv ye goat a light?"

A READER watched as a frail, bird-like woman got on the 44 bus into Glasgow from Newton Mearns only to be squashed against the window by her bulky husband who sat beside her and cheerily announced: "I bet you wish you married someone thinner!"

"I did," the woman tartly replied.

A READER thought the Glasgow ned on the late-night bus was perhaps just showing off a little too much when he told his mates that he had been stopped in Sauchiehall Street by police officers who wanted to search him and asked if he had anything sharp on him.

"Yes, a Hugo Boss jacket," he claimed he replied.

LOTHIAN BUSES has announced it is reverting to its old maroon livery for its fleet after changing ten years ago. It reminded Stewart MacKenzie of the Glasgow chap in the Edinburgh pub who asked a local: "What colour are your buses?"

"Maroon," he replied.

"Oh, thanks very much," said the Glaswegian, "I'll have a pint."

ALEX SMITH was at a bus stop in Glasgow waiting beside an obviously pregnant woman when a chap came up and asked: "Here, hen, when's it due?"

When she proudly replied: "Four months," it was obviously the moment he was waiting for as he replied: "Aw stuff it, ah'll walk instead," and strolled on by.

DOUGIE McNICOL in Bridge of Weir tells us about a friend who lost one of her shoes on the bus. No, it was not a drunken night out, but the fact that she has dressier shoes she wears at work, which she carries in a bag, and one of them had fallen out without her noticing.

After phoning the bus company, she was delighted to discover it had been handed in, and hubby was dispatched to the bus depot to collect it. When he entered the office and explained his mission, the chap behind the counter called to the back office: "Wullie, that's Cinderella's man here!"

ACCIDENTS that never happened in the past: A reader heard a young girl on the bus ask her pal why she had a black eye. "I was lying on my back texting," she replied, "when I dropped my phone."

A NUMBER of Glasgow bus stops now have electronic displays showing when the next bus is due to arrive.

Reader Dougie Lyden was reading such a display on Maryhill Road, which informed him that three buses were due in the next ten minutes, when an aged sage next to him declared: "Ah widnae pay too much heed tae that, son. They bus stoaps are famous for talkin' a loada s***e."

A READER hears a young girl on the bus into Glasgow explaining to her pal why she liked her job as a hairdresser. As the girl put it: "I love it. I get to talk about me all day long to everybody!"

A YOUNG girl on the 66 bus in Glasgow was telling her pal that she got a "big riddy" at the weekend when she saw a chap bending down and picking up fag ends from the street. As she explained: "Ma heart went out to him, so broke he had to smoke fag ends, so I handed him a couple of cigarettes from my packet.

"That's when he told me he worked in the shop, and had been sent out to sweep up."

DIANE STEWART tells us she was on a double-decker going in to Glasgow that was rammed with folk as the previous bus had failed to turn up. The driver, trying to clear some space, shouted out that there were "plenty of seats upstairs."

A passenger sitting at the top of the stairs shouted down: "Aye! But there's arses on all of them."

A READER on the bus into Glasgow from Baillieston heard one young girl say to her pal: "What's the difference between a lettuce and a cabbage?"

"I give in," replied her pal. "What is the difference?"

"No, I'm serious," said the first girl. "What's the difference?"

NOT EVERY Glaswegian is a charmer. Lesley O'Brien tells us she watched a wee grumpy bloke, trying to alight from a crowded bus at Gorbals, tell a rather large lady he was attempting to squeeze past: "Here, hen, swing yer belly tae the wan side."

A READER heard a wannabe comedian on a late night Glasgow bus who declared: "I've a neighbour I can't stand. He was banging on the wall so much at three in the morning I could hardly hear myself drill."

A READER tells us he was on a bus when he overheard two young chaps discussing health warnings on fag packets, with one declaring: "What does it mean, smokin' can make you impudent?"

And our reader thought to himself: "Actually, not far off the mark there."

A READER hears a chap on the bus tell his mate, whom he had not seen for a while, that he had recently been made redundant.

"Cheer up," replied the pal, "at least you won't have to go to some mingin' staff Christmas party this year."

# 3
# Battle of the Sexes

They say that women like the simple things in life – like men. Even after years of advice columns, and men getting in touch with their real feelings, relationships can still be a minefield. Here are a few of the mines.

"EVERY morning," said the loudmouth in the pub, "the newlywed guy next door kisses his young wife goodbye on the doorstep before going to work. So my wife says to me, 'Why don't you do that?' I wouldn't mind, I told her. But I hardly know the woman."

WEST of Scotland men have always had difficulty showing their emotion. One young lad having a beer with his pals in Glasgow's West End one Friday declared: "The only time I could get a hug from my dad was when I pretended to choke so that he would try the Heimlich manoeuvre on me."

A WOMAN on a train from Glasgow was explaining by mobile phone to her husband how he could make the spaghetti for tea. She made her travelling companions smile as she had to go right back to basics by telling him: "You boil the water in the kettle then put the pasta in the water."

The next night her friends on the train asked if the meal had gone well.

"No," she replied, "I got home to find the spaghetti sticking out of the kettle."

A READER tells us he was moaning to his wife about his forthcoming birthday, and asked her what was great about becoming thirty-nine. She told him that at least it would be the first time in his life that his age was greater than his waist size.

A GLASGOW reader tells us how impressed she was by her pal, arguing with her boyfriend on her mobile, who suddenly snapped the phone shut.

As she then sipped her wine, her phone rang, and everyone at the table could hear the now angry boyfriend shouting: "Did you just hang up on me?"

"I'm not sure," his girlfriend replied. "Did it sound like this?" and promptly shut her phone again.

TAM COWAN tells us about Fran, a friend from Perthshire, who was a country girl, though her husband was from Edinburgh. As she explained one day, wondering why folk were choking on their cups of tea: "Shug's very much a city boy – he hadn't even seen a cow until he met me."

A READER overhears a middle-aged woman in a Glasgow coffee shop tell her friends about her latest dating disaster. "I told him during the meal that he had something stuck between his teeth." After pausing, she added: "He then took them out to see what it was."

A READER was having her hair done in a Glasgow salon. The woman at the next seat was complaining to her hairdresser about her husband's lack of care and attention. Eventually the woman said to her hairdresser: "Do you think I should divorce him?"

The hairdresser thought about this before replying: "Oh, I think you should consult at least two hairdressers before taking a decision on that."

"I JOKED with the wife," said the loudmouth in the bar, "that she better not be tempted by all those good-looking instructors now that she's joined a gym. She told me not to worry. She said did I really think she'd still be living with me if she could pull one of them?"

"MY HUSBAND only stays with me because of the children," declared the woman having coffee with her friends in Glasgow. "Neither of them would let him move in with them."

A NEWTON MEARNS husband tells us he wasn't smart enough when his wife came home from a day's shopping with three new dresses.

"What do you want with three new dresses?" he blurted as she plonked the bags down.

"Three new pairs of shoes," she said as she got them out to show him.

"YOU KNOW that bit of a man that grows the more you stroke it?" said the woman having coffee with friends in Glasgow yesterday. "No, not that," she added when she saw their surprised looks. "His ego."

THE COURSE of true love doesn't always run smoothly, as a reader tells us of being on a train going in to Glasgow when a young chap sitting opposite told his pal: "She said she would think about going out with me if I got a job. So I told her, 'What makes you think I would want to go out with you if I had a job?'"

WHO SAYS romance is dead? A reader spotted a young chap grab a girl's hand in Glasgow's Buchanan Street and gently kiss it. He was saddened when she told the chap: "Hear, you! Are you kissin' ma haun or wiping yer nose?"

THE YOUNG woman draining a glass of cava on a Friday night in Glasgow was overheard telling her friends: "He's got a twenty-five-year mortgage on his flat, has had a season ticket to Ibrox for ten years, and has a five-year loan on his car. And then he tries to tell me he's afraid of commitment."

"NEVER date a woman whose father calls her Princess," said the loudmouth in the pub the other night. "Chances are she believes it."

WE HEARD about a chap wall-papering his front room who found it difficult putting up with his wife's frequent suggestions that he had left a bubble or two, or a strip of paper wasn't straight.

Seeing his fed-up coupon, she eventually told him: "The problem is that I'm a perfectionist and you're not."

He knows he really, really shouldn't have, but he couldn't help replying: "That's why you married me and I married you."


"AT WHAT point in an argument with your boyfriend," asked a woman having coffee with her friends, "would you ever say, 'OK, let's go on the *Jeremy Kyle Show* to resolve this'?"


A READER couldn't help but smile when he heard two women who had hammered the Jack Daniel's and Coke in a West-End bar discussing men, with the rather chubby one telling her stick-thin pal: "Men prefer to go to bed with women with a bit of meat on their bones."

"Oh, really?" her pal shot back with her eyebrows raised. "Did your boyfriend tell you that?"

"No," replied the large girl. "Yours did."


A READER tells us about his pal complaining to his wife that she was using the tumble dryer too much when the weather was fine, and she could hang the washing outside to dry and thus save electricity.

Rather than braining him with the tumble dryer, his wife agreed, and next day hung out the sheets on the line.

She is still laughing at the fact that when her husband went to bed in the freshly aired sheets, he leapt up shouting after being stung by a bee which had crawled inside them while they were hanging out.

A GLASGOW reader overheard a woman in a West-End bar being berated by her pal for dating a chap while seeing her previous boyfriend. "I wasn't cheating," her pal replied. "It was merely a relationship overlap."

"MY WIFE had a big argument with me," said the chap in the pub the other night. "She claimed I was a compulsive gambler, and she stormed off to her mother's."

He then added: "Two to one she's back by the weekend."

"I CALL my new boyfriend Malcolm X," said the woman having coffee with her friends in Glasgow's West End. "Not because he's a human rights activist, but because of the way he ends his affectionate texts to me."

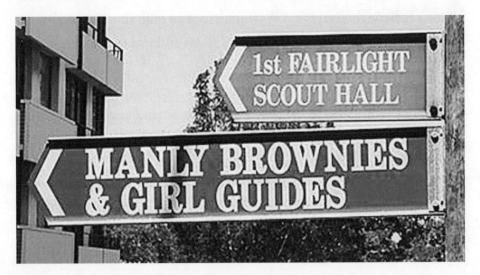

A WOMAN in a Glasgow coffee shop was asked by her pal if her husband helped with the housework. "Oh, aye," she replied. "His idea of helping is raising his legs when you're doing the hoovering."

A READER having coffee in Glasgow's city centre heard the woman at the next table bemoaning to friends that the daughter of a fellow friend was, in her opinion, too young to get married.

When her friends argued that perhaps she was old enough, the first woman argued: "They've got a PlayStation on their wedding list, for goodness sake."

"HAVE you ever noticed," said the chap in the pub, "that women's magazines only seem to have two main topics on their front pages – one, how disgusting all men are and, two, how to attract men?"

A GLASGOW reader claims the lad in Buchanan Street told his mate: "I don't believe that saying – 'A woman loves a man in uniform.' I went out three times in my McDonald's uniform and didn't pull once."

AN EAST KILBRIDE reader says he was sitting at home watching the telly when he heard his wife, in the kitchen, ask: "What would you like for dinner my sweetheart? Chicken, tuna or lamb?"

Cheered by that, he shouted back: "Lamb would be great."

But his wife replied: "You're having soup. I was talking to the cat."

"MY WIFE," said the loudmouth in the bar yesterday, "put on some sexy lingerie, asked me if I'd like to stay in bed and fool around with her all morning, and then said she would make me a fabulous lunch.

"I'm such an idiot, I fall for it every April 1."


"MY NEW boyfriend's a plastic surgeon," the thirty-something woman bragged to her pals on Friday night in a Glasgow cocktail bar. "Could you not get a real one?" one of her pals asked sweetly.


GLASWEGIANS can be so cruel. A reader catching a late train home watched as a young chap was being slagged by his mates about his new girlfriend. "People say she's very foxy," he said, defending his paramour.

"That's only because she rakes through the bins at night," a so-called pal hooted back.

# 4
# Having a Ball

**Football might divide a city with Glasgow's intense Rangers-Celtic rivalry. But there is no denying that interest in sport is a solid bond amongst people in our fast-changing world. These are a few of its stories.**

THE OLYMPIC TORCH for the London Olympics, it was announced, will go on a seventy-day tour of Britain, with organiser Lord Coe stating they would work with towns and cities to "ensure each community welcomes it in a way unique to their area".

Inevitably, an English commentator wonders whether they will use it to torch a car in Glasgow.

PARTICK THISTLE played a youthful Liverpool side for captain Alan Archibald's testimonial. After half-time, Thistle were first out the tunnel ready to get on with the second period and make up the one-goal deficit, but there was no sign of the Liverpool team.

"Why the delay?" asked one puzzled Jags fan.

It was very unkind of the fan behind him to declare: "They're in the Thistle dressing room going through wallets and looking for car keys."

GROWING in popularity this summer were triathlons where competitors swim, ride a bike, then finish with a foot race. A reader watching one such event in the Borders heard a fellow spectator shout the words of encouragement to a competitor who had just started the bike leg of the event: "Now ride that bike like you've just nicked it!"

RADIO CLYDE news editor Lorraine Herbison warned at an Epilepsy Scotland charity dinner in Glasgow of the dangers of live broadcasting. A colleague once informed the nation that a Celtic goalkeeper had: "pissed a late fatness test".

SURELY the Diary was above making fun of the England World Cup team's difficulties? Aye right. But as one philosopher told us: "Telling jokes about England isn't crossing the line – a referee told me that."

AND THANKS to many readers who told us that the England team flew home to a hero's welcome. The authorities made sure of it by diverting the plane to Glasgow.

AN EXASPERATED England fan argued: "No wonder Capello kept on claiming Rooney was scoring well in training – he was up against the England defence."

THERE was much debate about whether Scots should support England in the World Cup. Even ardent Scottish Nationalist and cartoonist Malky McCormack had an England flag flying outside his house in Waterside, Ayrshire.

A neighbour who went for a closer look tells us the flag had "Aye – that will be right" written on it.

THE VUVUZELAS, which make you think there's a giant wasp stuck in your telly, are not to everyone's taste. A reader heard a misogynist in the pub declare: "The World Cup is a lot like marriage. You know you're supposed to enjoy it, but there's a constant droning noise in the background."

BUT AN English fan managed to get a dig in at us neutrals north of the border. "The England-USA game showed us what it would be like if we had a Great Britain football team in the Olympics – an England side with a Scottish goalkeeper."

AND ANOTHER English fan made the point: "At the World Cup there's a thin line between success and failure." He then added: "It's called Hadrian's Wall."

CONGRATULATIONS to outgoing Rangers player DaMarcus Beasley making the USA's World Cup squad. A Rangers fan tells us there was some debate, when Beasley joined the club, over whether he was worth the £700,000 paid for him. A fan of the player watching him at Ibrox said supportively: "In a couple of seasons, five million won't buy him."

"And I'm one of them," piped up a fan further along the row.

NORTH KOREAN Supreme Leader Kim Jong-il, banned live coverage of his country's early World Cup matches on state television. "If only we had thought of that during the qualifying stages," a member of the Tartan Army tells us.

JUST to rub it in to Scotland fans, even New Zealand, famous for the oval ball and not the round variety, qualified for the World Cup finals.

Their only other final was Spain 1982, when the chairman of New Zealand Soccer was ex-pat Glaswegian Charlie Dempsey. Antipodean correspondent Gary Johnson tells us that when the largely amateur squad boarded the plane to the finals and scrambled for seats in economy, Charlie's last-minute pep talk was: "Remember, lads, my heart is with you – every step of the way.

"My arse, on the other hand," he continued, "won't be, since I'm sitting in first class."

THERE was much debate about David Murray's attempts to sell Rangers. One Celtic fan phoned to tell us that Asian entrepreneur Satty Singh, a Rangers supporter and owner of the Mearns Castle Golf Academy, was going into partnership with current major Rangers shareholder, South African businessman Dave King, to buy the club. We waited patiently for the punch line.

"The new company will be called," he added, "the Singh King Ship."

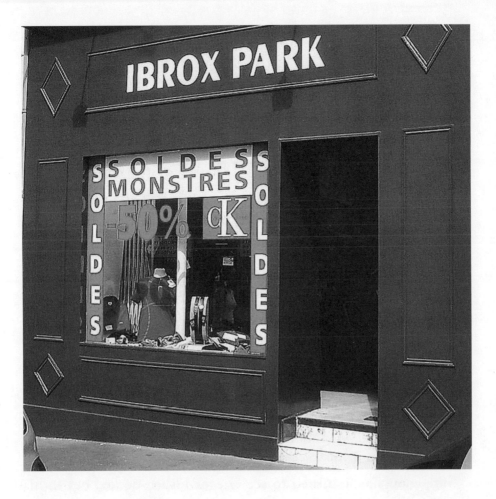

THE CHAP in the golf club after the first day of the Masters looked at the leader board on the telly and declared: "Will Tiger never stop his bad behaviour? I see he's chasing after Couples now."

A READER who ventured into a Partick bookie to place some World Cup bets was halted by an altercation at the desk where a chap was having a dispute over a bet. "I've been coming here all my life!" the old fella declared, hoping for sympathy.

"We've only been open two years," the not-for-moving assistant replied.

ROYAL ASCOT reminded us of the comedian who declared: "I saw one race at Royal Ascot." He added: "Rich white people."

AFTER Rangers lost 4-1 to St Johnstone, Scottish Television was told that a group of Rangers fans was protesting outside a pub in Govan. Hoping for dramatic pictures of effigies and scarves being burned by the mob, a reporter and cameraperson were dispatched.

An embarrassed reporter returned to say that she had managed to find the pub all right, and saw the gathered throng. When she approached to start interviewing the punters, she was stopped by a police officer who asked what she was doing.

"Filming the protest," she replied.

To which the officer responded: "This is no protest. This is a film set for the new episode of *Rab C Nesbitt*."

Sure enough, she turned to see Gregor Fisher, decked out in his iconic string vest and headband.

A READER overheard two chaps on the train into Glasgow discussing sport, with one declaring: "When I was at school, we had to play rugby. So when I had the chance to play football I grabbed it with both hands."

"So not much change there, then," thought our reader.

THE HERALD news story that claimed sectarianism still existed in the workplace reminded Willie Gibson of the speaker at Grangemouth Golf Club who declared that the definition of an atheist in Glasgow was someone who went to a Rangers v Celtic game just to watch the football.

MOTHERWELL FC, stung by critics who claimed its pitch last season was more suited to planting potatoes than silky football, announced it was being re-turfed. One fan commented on a website: "Don't forget – it's green side up this time."

FORMER police inspector, now author, Les Brown, heard some chaps in the pub discussing investigations into alleged match fixing in snooker. "I can foresee in the future," remarked one of them. "A sports announcer saying, 'The final of the UK Championships takes place tomorrow. If you don't want to know the result, look away now'."

CAVALIER footballer of many clubs, Chic Charnley, at the launch of his book *Seeing Red*, was asked if he would have liked to have earned the fantastic sums professionals are now paid. Refreshingly, Chic said no, because of the temptations. As he put it: "My friend Brian Gallacher and I discussed this and reckoned if we had that kind of cash it would be like the oil rigs – two weeks on and two weeks off – on the batter."

WHEN the fitba' season was over, it didn't stop John Daly from telling us: "Overheard in my local was the punter wondering if Rangers are fined by the taxman, as is being mooted, will this be the first time Rangers will have been given a penalty they deserve?"

EVEN natural disasters attract Old Firm gags. "Apparently the dust cloud closing Glasgow Airport had nothing to do with a volcano," said a caller to the Diary. "It was just Celtic's trophy room being cleaned."

OUR GOLF gags to mark the return of golfers reminds Bob Jarvie of the golfer asking the club pro for advice. "The pro asked him to hit a few balls before commenting. He then told him the best advice he could give him was to cut a foot off his clubs," Bob tells us. "'Will that help my game?' asked the player. 'No,' said the pro. 'But they'll go in the bin easier'."

CLAIMS of biased refereeing in Scotland remind former Ayr United captain Johnny Graham of playing against Rangers, and upbraiding the linesman for giving all the offside decisions in favour of the Glasgow side.

Later, when Johnny took a corner and hoisted the ball straight out of play, the linesman standing beside him at the corner flag merely commented: "And you say I'm having a bad game?"

TALKING of referees, Tom Hamilton tells us of the late Willie McClure, deputy head at Prestwick Academy, a keen amateur footballer with no bookings who transgressed when he told a referee that he was "myopic".

The ref replied: "Son, I don't know what it means, but your name's going in the book."

AFTER the disappointing Winter Olympics for Great Britain, John Duffy reads the headline on the BBC website "GB men's curlers out after defeat" and thinks to himself that it's nice to get your hair done to cheer yourself up after a disappointment.

FALKIRK'S relegation from the SPL was not mourned by everyone. A Stenhousemuir football fan claims the local newspaper reported: "Players from Falkirk FC visited the local children's hospital over the Christmas period.

"'It's very rewarding to put a smile back on the faces of those suffering adversity and an uphill struggle,' said Scott McGovern, aged eight."

"TIGER WOODS," says a reader, "was at least honest when his wife asked him where he was going and he simply said he was going to play a round."

JIM DOCHERTY in Ruislip was watching a rugby match in the London League when a rather posh-accented captain of one side approached the ref and declared: "Referee, are you aware that you have awarded ten penalties against us and given us none?"

In a gruff Scottish accent, the ref replied: "Naw, you're wrang. It's now eleven, so get back ten metres before it's twelve."

Thus ended the conversation.

NEWSPAPER websites are always wary about Old Firm fans hijacking the online discussions in order to make vituperative comments about the opposition.

That doesn't stop the fans from trying though.

We can only assume, then, that it was a Rangers fan who commented on another newspaper's story about Tom Daley's world diving title that the fifteen-year-old must have been good "to beat Larsson of Sweden, Petrov of Bulgaria and Nakamura of Japan".

READER John Sleith was at the Motherwell-Flamurtari Europa cup tie, which was being played at Airdrie United's ground as Motherwell's park was being relaid.

As Motherwell went in to a historic six-nil lead at half-time, he heard a fellow Motherwell fan point to the hundred or so dejected Albanian fans in the crowd, and opine: "Wait till they realise that all they've got to look forward to console themselves afterwards is a night out in Airdrie."

GOOD news for Afghanistan, where the country's cricket side qualified for the Twenty20 World Cup, the lively contest so named as both sides play only twenty overs each. We are told that when an American official in Afghanistan was told the news, he replied: "Well, at least they've got ten years to prepare for it."

READER Dave Johnston in Garelochhead was much taken with the interview with Aberdeen owner Stewart Milne commenting on manager Mark McGhee being spat at by his own supporters. As Stewart said, he admired McGhee "for taking it on the chin".

SAY NO TO RANGERS

THE SCOTTISH Junior Cup final between Linlithgow Rose and Largs Thistle was the usual tousy affair. However, Linlithgow fielded Spanish left-back Jorge Virgili, which makes us pretty certain that the phrase uttered by a fan at the game: "Aye, he was with Barcelona as a teenager," has never been spoken at a Junior Cup final before.

WE MENTIONED Motherwell Football Club getting some stick for the state of its pitch, despite spending thousands on upgrading it in the summer. Perhaps labouring the point was the Hibs fan who, after seeing how much sand had been spread on the pitch, went up to the Ladbrokes betting stall in the east stand and asked: "What are the odds for the camel racing?"

TIGER WOODS' wife taking a golf club to the car window reminds us of the gag about police being called to a house where a husband was holding a five-iron over the lifeless body of his wife.

When he confirmed under questioning that he had struck her with the club, the officer asked: "How many times?"

The golfer replied: "Maybe six, seven times. But just put me down for a four."

DO WE believe the caller who claims that Rangers fans are now singing to their traditional "Follow Follow" tune: "Borrow, borrow, we will borrow millions."

IRVINE MEADOW'S glamour cup tie with Hibs reminded a fan in Ayrshire of when Meadow were at home to Glenafton, and a Glenafton official climbed over the wall to give the linesman some angry "advice".

The linesman complained to the referee, and the sole police officer on duty strolled over to the Glenafton official and told him: "If you approach that linesman again, I will be forced to arrest you. However, should you wish to assault that useless referee, I'll help you."

A DIARY story about TV chef Keith Floyd insisting that a young *Herald* features writer have a gin while interviewing him reminds public relations executive Moyra Peffer of her fledgling days when she had a meeting at 11am with a well-known Scottish football manager.

Offered a refreshment, she asked for an orange juice. Despite the earliness of the hour, he asked her with typical Scottish male generosity: "Do ye no' want a wee vodka in that, hen?"

# 5
# Working at the Chalk Face

**Another common experience that binds all Scots is their school days, whether fondly remembered or hated. These are the tales.**

AT THE last week of school, pupils become a bit boisterous. One teacher in a Glasgow South-Side secondary appealed to a noisy third year class to be quiet, and as it took some time for them to settle down, he told them: "You know, sometimes I feel invisible."

"Who said that?" piped up a voice from the back of the class.

A TEACHER at Johnstone High School was about to intervene when he overheard a third-year boy ask his mate: "How faur huv you gaun wi' a lassie?" But he breathed a sigh of relief when the pal replied after a few seconds thought: "Paisley."

BOB BYIERS recalls when his children were at primary school and a classmate wrote in her news book about her mummy's tights falling into the soup from the clothes-drying pulley above the kitchen table.

"The poor wee girl," says Bob, "had not yet learned that there was a silent 'gh' in tights."

A GLASGOW teacher tells us, while discussing the human body, she asked her class if anyone had ever broken a bone. One wee lad put his hand up, and she asked him if it had hurt. He replied: "No."

Thinking he was just trying to be brave in front of his classmates, she then asked which bone.

"Ma sister's arm," he replied.

A TEACHER tells us she was asking her class why mobile phone masts could be bad for your health. After a lengthy pause, one chap hesitantly answered: "You might walk into it?"

AT A WEST of Scotland school, a teacher tells us a first-year pupil was stopped by a colleague and asked why he wasn't wearing his school tie. He claimed his dog, a Rottweiler, had eaten it.

"For goodness sake," the annoyed teacher told him, "why were you using your tie to play with a Rottweiler?"

"Please, sir, I wasn't," the lad replied. "I was wearing it at the time."

CHRIS BURT from Falkirk tells us about a group of mums waiting at the primary school gate when one of the little ones came out in a blazer that was clearly too big for him.

The perplexed little lad then shouted out: "Haw, maw! Someone's nicked ma Polos – and left me 10p and a hankie."

THE RESURGENCE in teaching Scottish history has its pitfalls. A Glasgow teacher tells us he was discussing the first Battle of Falkirk with his class when one lippy pupil piped up: "I don't know what Falkirk was like in 1298, but I was there last weekend and didn't think it was worth fighting over."

A GLASGOW primary teacher discussing clocks with her class asked one lad: "If you go to your gran's at 1.15, and go home at 2.45, how long have you been there?"

She was impressed when he thought about this for a while, then answered: "Not long, miss."

TALES of teachers meeting former pupils reminds reader Brian Maule, a former Hutchie pupil, of telling his teachers that he was going to study medicine. A year later he had a Saturday job as a butcher's delivery boy and was loading the van when a former teacher came up and declared: "Well Maule, at least you've managed to get a white coat."

TEACHERS meeting former pupils continued. Duncan Robinson, in the West Dunbartonshire constituency Labour Party, tells us that local MP John McFall, a former teacher, was on a visit to Barlinnie prison in Glasgow when he was stopped by an inmate who said: "Hi, Mr McFall. Remember me fae school? You were my guidance teacher."

OUR TALES of former pupils meeting teachers remind Joe O'Rourke of the classmate at his school many years ago who just liked staring out of the window. Says Joe: "The teacher used to shout at him, 'You'll never get a job looking out the window all day!'

"Well, she got that completely wrong – he was a bus driver for thirty years."

EDDIE McFADDEN tells us about his brother-in-law some years back, stacking shelves in B&Q in Motherwell, when his carefully arranged display collapsed.

Continued Eddie: "A voice from behind said, 'Bet you wish you'd paid more attention at school, eh?' and he turned round to discover one of his old teachers standing there with a smug grin on his face.

"He was too gobsmacked to inform the teacher that he only worked there on Saturdays as he was at university from Monday to Friday."

A TEACHER tells us she is still smarting from going over present, future and past tenses with her class and asking: "What tense is the sentence, 'I am beautiful'?"

Inevitably, the class clown shouted out: "Past tense."

A HAMILTON reader tells us that the minister was talking to her daughter's primary class about Easter and asked the seven-year-olds why Jesus died on the cross.

Expecting an answer along the lines of: "So we'd all be saved," he was left temporarily speechless when one of the sweet-faced tots replied: "He bled to death."

A NEWTON MEARNS reader watched two schoolgirls brush their teeth as they walked down the Ayr Road after school. She was thinking to herself how good of them to be so careful with their molars after perhaps consuming some sweets, when she then saw one of them stub a fag out on the pavement.

JIM MacEWAN in Nethy Bridge tells us about his wife teaching in an Aberdeen primary where stories were being written about cavemen. One girl's essay had a small spelling error.

"They had very little comfort, just a little rough matting on the floor," with only one T in matting. Or at least his wife assumed it was a spelling error.

RETIRED teacher John Hodgson tells us of a primary school colleague who, attempting to make arithmetic more relevant, asked: "If I had ten oranges in one hand and seven oranges in the other, what would I have?"

"Big hauns, miss," came the reply.

A PUPIL sitting outside the office at a West Dunbartonshire school was heard asking the girl next to him: "Who ur you waitin' fur?"

The girl replied: "Ma big sister is collecting me. They couldn't contact ma Mum, she is oot wi' her personal trainer."

The young lad thought about this before asking: "Is that like a social worker?"

WHEN school sports days started, we were told of one Lanarkshire school where the timetable of races was being discussed. A student teacher suddenly asked, when told there was a wheelbarrow race, where would they get the wheelbarrows.

IT GLADDENS the heart to see all these happy children skipping off to a new school year. But one teacher isn't as full of the joys of life. She tells us: "I opened a book I was marking in my class the other day to find that in the absence of a glue stick a child had used a bogie to stick his work down."

A MOTHER tells us her stomach flipped when her twelve-year-old daughter came home from school and declared: "Boys are only interested in one thing."

A feeling of relief followed though when the daughter added: "PlayStations."

AN AYRSHIRE school planning a skiing trip for its senior pupils was impressing upon the older lads that any attempt at under-age drinking on the jaunt would be severely frowned upon.

Staff didn't know whether to be happy or sad when one seventeen-year-old was emphatic that no attempt would be made to access drink during the trip, then added: "Certainly not after that hangover I had last weekend."

A MUM tells us she pointed out to her little one as he was getting his school shoes on: "You've got a hole in your sock."

"How else would I get my foot in it?" he replied in confusion.

TEACHER Debbie Meehan tells us that she always says to her Higher maths class how clever they are, and how high her expectations are for them in future exams.

When a pupil asked why she said that, she told them that there was evidence that if you say these encouraging things to people often enough, it becomes a reality.

One of the class immediately exclaimed: "Miss, you're a great teacher."

A PARENT at her daughter's school's parents' night – yes, an impressive use of apostrophes there – was flicking idly through her child's essay book when she noticed that she had misspelled "rain" as "rane".

Her daughter's teacher was clearly quite amused by that, as she had written in the margin: "This is one of the worst spells of rain we've had in a long time."

A GLASGOW chemistry teacher tells us he fears one of his pupils may not be too excited by the subject. He noticed on the pupil's jotter that the lad had neatly stuck on the cover, below the word Chemistry, a label from a bottle of medicine. It read: "Warning. May cause nausea and extreme drowsiness."

ONE YOUNGSTER, on hearing that VAT was going up to twenty percent, told his parents: "But on the plus side, some of my maths questions are going to be a lot easier to work out."

AN EAGLESHAM reader tells us that when he was at school, the teacher asked the class the best way to keep milk fresh and a fellow pupil replied: "Keep it in the cow."

# 6
# The Knife of Stanley

**Being arrested, they say, is no laughing matter. But sometimes it is.**

JAMES FRASER tells us about a report filed in the old Partick police office in Glasgow by a probationer who stated that a house fire had been caused by an electrical fitting falling from the ceiling and igniting the carpet below.

A more senior officer reading the report thought this sounded so unusual that he phoned the fire station to check. There was much laughter at the police station when the firefighter looked at his records and explained that the fire had been caused by a dropped light.

A READER was at Greenock Sheriff Court where a case involved an affray in a local restaurant. A diner, who appeared as a witness, was asked by the fiscal: "Were you there on a date?"

"No," the chap replied. "I was with the wife."

A RETIRED police officer tells us they arrested a young chap for car theft, but as he appeared to be under the influence of drink or drugs they asked the police doctor to have a look at him.

In the cell, the doctor gave the confused chap a shake and asked him: "I'm a doctor. Did you take anything?"

The befuddled chap replied: "A Peugeot 207."

"I WAS stopped by a traffic cop," said the loudmouth in the pub. "He came up and asked me, 'Do you know why I stopped you, sir?' So I told him, 'Well, if you can't remember, I'm not going to remind you.'"

A READER tells us about the Glasgow defendant, pleading guilty to slashing someone in a street affray, whose lawyer was overcome with verbosity and told the sheriff: "My client realises that the Sword of Damocles is hanging over him but I would ask for leniency."

The sheriff merely replied: "It's not the Sword of Damocles that concerns me in this case but the Knife of Stanley."

JIM SCOTT in Midlothian tells us about a pal who was a sales rep for a steel company during the Falklands War. He was stopped en route from Glasgow to Yorkshire for speeding.

Says Jim: "He told them he had an urgent component for the Royal Naval Dockyard at Devonport, and that was why he was speeding. He opened his boot to show the officers a part he had picked up from a customer, thinking they would let him go on his way with no ticket.

"Instead, they escorted him to the county border where he was met by another patrol car who then escorted him to Warwickshire, where again he was met by another car, which continued all the way to Devonport.

"He then phoned his wife to try to explain why he was further away from home than he had been seven hours earlier."

AFTER Justice Minister Kenny MacAskill was in Dundee's Whitfield estate making a speech on recovering goods from criminal gangs, a police officer recalled a related story. He told us about the time his police football team was playing in Whitfield, one of the more challenging housing schemes, and having been told there had been robberies from the changing rooms, decided to keep all their valuables locked in their minivan when they played. The van was nicked.

AN EDINBURGH reader tells us he attended a business dinner where a chap at his table, after a few libations, launched into a lengthy tale about suing a company, but the case got tied up in the courts. Our reader thought it was going to be awkward when the chap ended his story belligerently with: "In the end, the only people who got any money were the bloody lawyers!" as there were a couple of lawyers at the table.

He didn't have to worry, as one of the lawyers filled the ensuing silence by opining: "Oh, I do like a story with a happy ending."

ROBERT HAYES tells us of the officers who stopped in the genteel suburb of Newton Mearns where a car was marooned at traffic lights. When they approached the driver, he told them: "Thank goodness you're here. I appear to have broken down in a rather awkward place. Could you give me a little push?"

Perhaps it was the chap's imperious manner, but one of the constables couldn't resist stepping up and gently pushing the gent on his upper chest.

They did then move his car, but the driver still turned up at the police station later to complain.

OUR MENTION of Paisley Sheriff Court reminds a reader of being in that same place when a chap was pleading guilty to a breach of the peace. The accused then caused a bit of confusion about his plea when he added: "I was too drunk to remember what happened – but it sounds like the sort of thing I would do."

OUR STORY of how motorists deal with traffic cops reminds John Daly in Houston of a Norwegian visitor to the then British Steel Clydebridge works at Cambuslang, who admitted to hammering down the M73 in a hired car.

He was stopped by traffic officers who, when he was pulled over and wound his window down, asked him: "Having difficulty taking off, sir?"

A FORMER Strathclyde traffic officer tells us of the cheekiest motorist he ever stopped. After flagging down a driver who went through a red light, the police officer asked him: "Didn't you see the red light?"

"The light, yes," the driver replied. "But you? No."

TALES of jaikies remind a reader of the legendary Sheriff J Irvine Smith who, when on the bench in Greenock, regularly had to deal with a recidivist named Barney Noone who showed off his misplaced intellect by always addressing the bench in verse.

Sheriff Smith thus prepared himself for Barney's next inevitable appearance and after Barney recited some verse in mitigation, the sheriff replied: "Thirty days hath November, April, June and Barney Noone"

AND, OF COURSE, there is the oft-quoted tale of Sheriff Smith on a busy Monday after a rowdy weekend sentencing numerous accused before him to prison terms.

An official asked him to go easy, as they had run out of space on the transport to Barlinnie.

"Here," said the sheriff throwing over the Yellow Pages. "You'll find it under coach hire."

OUR TALES of Sheriff J Irvine Smith remind Alun Hotchkiss in Luxembourg of attending a Radio Westsound Burns Supper when Sheriff Smith, proposing the Immortal Memory, introduced himself as "the Messiah". He then added: "I must be, as only this morning a miscreant led into the dock looked up at the bench and muttered, 'It's him! Jesus Christ!'"

JOURNALIST Alan Fisher, now with the Al Jazeera news network, was once covering the High Court in Aberdeen for Northsound Radio when a witness was asked if she saw the person responsible for the crime.

Says Alan: "My heart sank as she pointed in my direction with the classic: 'Aye there he is there.'

"It was enough to cause a small uproar in the court. Just as things were dying down, it erupted again when one of the five accused turned round and said, 'We were wi' him.'"

A FORMER police officer of many years ago in Glasgow was at the sheriff court when the sheriff told the accused that if there had been a shred of evidence against him, he would have been sentenced to six months, as opposed to the three months he was getting.

OUR SHERIFF court stories remind journalist Alistair Nicol of when he was a young reporter for the West Lothian Courier covering Linlithgow Sheriff Court. A visiting cross-eyed sheriff was dealing with three ne'er-do-wells in the dock.

Says Alistair: "The sheriff looked at the first one and asked, 'How do you plead?' The second one said, 'Not guilty.' The sheriff said, 'I wasn't talking to you.' The third one said, 'I never said a word!'"

AN EDINBURGH reader tells us her friend got a job teaching English to prisoners, and is still blushing after asking her first class: "Now do you all know what a sentence is?"

A READER watching the Scottish news on the telly with the subtitles on saw it reported that Scottish Justice Secretary Kenny MacAskill had gone to visit "my granny" in Greenock prison, and thought: "What a kind grandson, but why are they making such a fuss about it?"

RODDY MACLEAN on Lewis says that when Stornoway got its first set of traffic lights in the eighties, an elderly chap from rural Lewis drove in for his annual shopping and went straight through the red light, narrowly missing an old dear on her zimmer.

When the cops stopped him and asked if he saw the lights, he innocently replied: "Oh, aye. They're ferry nice."

GLASGOW lawyers Professor Leo Martin and Stephen Giusti are perhaps not as trim as they were in their younger days. But it was surely unfair of a fellow lawyer, when they told him they were moving to a new office in Blythswood Street above an award-winning Glasgow restaurant, to declare: "How often do you get two fat lawyers above Two Fat Ladies?"

WOMEN drivers. Bless. Ivor Taylor tells us about driving along Nithsdale Road where oncoming motorists flashed their lights at him. Ivor slowed down and, sure enough, around the corner was a police speed trap, which he smugly drove past, although he noticed the woman driver behind him pulled in to the side without being asked to. He later met the woman and asked why she stopped. "I saw all the drivers flashing their lights at me, so when I saw the police I stopped to ask them why they thought people were doing that," she explained.

OUR story about the prison English teacher who asked if the class knew what a sentence was reminded a teacher in East Ayrshire of asking a pupil what his big brother, whom she had previously taught, was doing. "Six months," he replied.

A READER in Glasgow's George Square watched as an attractive blonde was pulled over by police for driving in a bus lane. She told the officer that it was the fault of other drivers who wouldn't let her pull into the main stream of traffic.

"I'm sure somebody would have let you in with that winning smile," argued the gallant police officer.

But not to be beaten, the blonde merely pointed at her windscreen and said: "Tinted windows."

DRUMMOND SMALL recalls a friend returning home from evening class in Glasgow with a boxed set of knives, which he needed for his course on meat inspection. Stopped in Central Station by police officers, he was asked why he was carrying knives in public.

For some reason he thought it was smart to blurt out: "For cutting up side streets."

WHEN Pete Sinclair moved to Chicago, he was pulled over by an officer who told him he had crossed the median. Pete's reply – "I didn't know the equator ran through Chicago" – earned him a $35 ticket.

THE SCAFFOLDING has come down from the Britannia Panopticon on Glasgow's Argyle Street after sandstone cleaning.

Irene Graham, chair of the Panopticon Trust, which is preserving the old music hall, is delighted, not only because it means people can see the building in all its glory, but also because it stops sneak thieves who have been using the scaffolding to break into the auditorium.

She tells us: "One cheeky thief thought he'd fool the local constabulary by posing as a dummy alongside the Victoriana-clad mannequins which are dotted about the balcony and auditorium.

"Sadly for him, his tracksuit and trainers gave him away."

TWO GLASGOW lawyers in Paris for rugby's Heineken Cup final made the front of a long queue to buy train tickets at Charles de Gaulle airport when they were approached by an American tourist who offered them €1 if they would buy his ticket, too. He was told that for €1 the best advice he was getting was to join the back of the queue.

# 7
# Home Like River City

Women are more independent than ever before. As actress Elaine C Smith explained it, we shouldn't be downhearted about the women curlers in the Winter Olympics not repeating their gold medal success of 2002.

Said Elaine: "Eight years ago Scottish women had plenty of practice sweeping around a deadweight.

"Now they've divorced the deadweight and are having a good time."

"DID YOU see that the Iranian government has banned the mullet hairstyle?" said the woman having coffee with her friends.

"Goodness," replied her pal. "Cumnock will be breaking off diplomatic relations then."

A FALKIRK reader heard a female stopping a pal in the High Street and telling her: "Did you hear that Margaret's just had her second husband cremated?"

"Aye, Ah know," replied her pal. "Some of us cannae find a husband, and others have husbands to burn."

WOMEN falling out – it's never a pretty sight. We fear a drink or two had been taken in the west end bar when one woman out with pals took exception to something said by one of them and replied: "I was going to give you a nasty look – but I see you already have one."

A READER tells us her friend looked up from her glass of wine in the cocktail bar last week and declared: "My great fear is that there is no such thing as PMS, and it's just my personality."

"I DON'T know what all the fuss is about genetically modified food," said the woman having coffee with her friends.
  "I had a lovely leg of salmon the other day."

OVER 10,000 women have joined the Facebook page "Going out like *Sex in the City*, coming home like *River City*" – a reference to the comparisons between the glamorous New York-based TV series, and the plainer fare of BBC Scotland's soap opera filmed in Dumbarton.
  But as one of the women on the site wailed: "I go out like *River City*, and think I'm like *Sex in the City* by the end of the night."

"I WAS lying on the couch watching *Saturday Kitchen*," said the woman having coffee with friends, "when hubby walked in and told me, 'What are you watching that for? You rarely cook.'

"So I asked him why he watched *Match of the Day* as it's years since he could run the length of a football pitch."

BEWARE of taking on older women. A young woman at a recent works night out in the west end cattily told an older colleague: "You need to be younger to dance to that song." She merely replied: "And you need to be prettier to wear a dress like that."

TALKING of the west end, a reader heard a woman entering a well-known bar there say to her pal: "Every time I walk in here I remember my mother's wise words.

"She said, 'Don't pick that up, you don't know where it's been.'"

WE OVERHEAR a Glasgow woman arguing that a mutual friend's boyfriend was a tad on the short side. Or as she declared: "Small? Put it this way, when it rains, he's the last to know."

A READER passing the Blood Transfusion Centre in Glasgow heard a woman say to her pal: "Shall we go and give blood?"

When her friend asked why, she replied: "It should make us a couple of pounds lighter for Weight Watchers tonight."

YES, THERE are lots of sharp women out there. A reader tells us he was in a city centre barber's when the girl cutting the chap next to him asked in time-honoured tradition: "Are you going anywhere nice for your holidays?"

"Yes, I'm going to Guantanamo Bay," replied the customer.

"That'll be nice," replied the hairdresser. "And will there be any other smart alecks there?"

A MIDDLE-AGED reader went to her GP with a very sore throat, and when she arrived at the surgery, the receptionist asked for her date of birth. In a barely audible whisper, she told the receptionist her fifties date. The receptionist whispered back: "It's OK, I'm not going to tell anyone."

A NEWTON MEARNS reader confides to us she was putting face cream on when her little son asked why she was doing it. "To make myself look beautiful," she replied.

Minutes later when she was removing the cream, her little one, who had not stopped staring at her, asked: "Giving up?"

AN EDINBURGH reader tells us that the woman having coffee with her friends in George Street at the table next to him declared that a mutual friend was so dense, "she would think a radiator was a house-warming present".

# 8
## I'm Fair Hank Marvin

**Scots can be a bit cynical about celebrities – unless they can make a joke about them.**

ACTOR John Barrowman, in Glasgow to promote his pantomime *Aladdin* at the SECC, met pupils from his old primary, Mount Vernon, who told him his teacher Mrs McFarlane, although retired, was still alive.

He made an exaggerated motion of licking the palm of his hand and told them: "Just before the class picture, she licked her hand and pushed my hair down. And they wonder why I don't like women . . ."

DUNDEE is perhaps not the richest of areas in the country. John McCann tells us: "Comedian Emo Philips, when he was at the Fringe a few years ago, told the audience, 'I love going to Dundee, spending a £20 note, and watching it ripple through the economy like a donkey swallowed by an anaconda'."

A READER swears he was in a pub in Glasgow's east end where the discussion turned to TV celebrities, and a local chipped in with: "I was on the telly once.

"Well, not me exactly, but an artist's sketch of me."

OUR SHOWBIZ correspondent phones to tell us that Katie Price's husband, cage-fighter Alex Reid, had won his first fight since their marriage. "The budgie never knew what hit it," he added.

A MILNGAVIE reader was at the hairdresser's when she told the young stylist that she was looking forward to going to see Cliff Richard and the Shadows now that they had reunited for a series of concerts.

The young stylist asked who the Shadows were.

Our surprised reader asked: "Surely you've heard of Hank Marvin?"

The young girl thought about that for a moment before telling her: "He's a real person? I thought that it was just a saying for when you were hungry."

ENTERTAINER Rory Bremner, speaking at the opening of the rebranded Dunblane Hydro, said he had recently been at a function with easyJet founder Stelios Haji-Ioannou.

"Afterwards we shared a taxi," said Rory. "Stelios opened the door and said, 'After you.'

"He then charged me £10 for priority boarding."

GLASGOW Airport terror attack icon, cigarette-smoking baggage handler John Smeaton, revealed at a show in Glasgow his philosophy that if he saw a polis being attacked, he would go and help him.

The point was perhaps spoiled by an audience member interrupting: "I'm frae the Gallowgate and if I see a polisman being attacked, I'd be right in there giving him a kicking, too."

Incidentally, John explained why he was having a fag outside the airport at the time of the attack: he was calming his nerves before having to tell his supervisor that he hadn't loaded golf clubs in time for the Malaga flight which had gone off with the golfers on board.

AWARD-WINNING composer and conductor Sir Peter Maxwell Davies told an audience at Glasgow Royal Concert Hall that while giving a concert in Las Vegas, he sat in his hotel room waiting for a telephone interview, which had been scheduled with a newspaper, but he never got the call.

He later learned that the journalist had been told that there was no one of that name listed. When the journalist insisted that Sir Peter was a very important conductor, the hotel staff member told him: "If he was that important, he wouldn't be staying at this hotel."

It later transpired that the hotel's computer couldn't cope with such a long name and simply abbreviated it to Mavis.

Sir Peter has since written a piece entitled "Mavis in Las Vegas".

ENTREPRENEUR Charan Gill, formerly of Ashoka fame, re-entered the restaurant business by opening the sumptuous

Slumdog restaurant in Glasgow's Sauchiehall Street. Charan was immaculately turned out in an expensive jacket with bold colourful stripes for the opening, but such sartorial elegance is not always appreciated.

A late arrival at Slumdog, who asked where he could find Charan, was simply told by a fellow guest: "Look for a deckchair wi' two legs."

RADIO SCOTLAND'S Fred MacAulay, just back from the Kilkenny Comedy Festival, told us he commentated on the comedians' Ireland v Rest of the World charity football match. When rising Scottish star Kevin Bridges put himself in the middle of a defensive wall, Fred could be heard telling the crowd: "Kevin's a Clydebank boy. So it's rare for him to see a wall and not urinate against it."

AND FRED on stage is not the cuddly character from his Radio Scotland show. When one woman at a show took his photograph, Fred told her: "You're from Greenock? If you scroll back the pictures on that digital camera, you'll eventually find whose it is."

OUR MENTION of Greenock brought forth from David Scott the surely erroneous claim: "Greenock: a town that's not twinned with anywhere else in the world – but does have a suicide pact with Dundee."

WE CAN'T believe it's twenty years since we crowded around the telly to see Nelson Mandela being released from jail.

The Diary, of course, took a less reverential view at the time by asking people what they thought Mandela's first words were on his release. Our favourite was: "Did Kilmarnock really win the league in 1965?"

THE GREAT Chic Murray's daughter Annabelle tells us of when she was interviewed over the phone by a London-based newspaper about her late father, and she stated: "Chic was a master of absurdities, but never smutty."

To her horror, she was then mistakenly quoted as giving the wonderful oxymoron: "Chic was a master of obscenities, but never smutty."

SCREENPLAY writer Peter McDougall was recalling the film on Glasgow murderer turned sculptor Jimmy Boyle, *A Sense of Freedom*. A mock-up of a pub had to be built in the east end of Glasgow to film scenes. A local hard-man wandered in and ordered a pint. The actor barman explained it was not a real pub, but a film set.

The chap thought about this, and naturally came to the conclusion the barman was taking the mickey – and decked him.

OWL CITY were number one in the charts with "Fireflies". Adam Young from Minnesota, who formed the group, explained the name Owl City came "from a wee incident I had in Scotland".

He continued: "I used to visit my wonderful creaky grandmother in Edinburgh, and I happened to be waltzing scot-free through the lovely Scottish foothills when I suddenly came upon a forest that was literally crammed full of owls. Big owls, small owls, fat owls, skinny owls, tough owls, sissy owls ... you name it. It was literally a city of owls."

But before Alex Salmond names him as an honorary Scot, we

should point out that Adam changes the reason why he calls his band Owl City in every interview. But we still reckon the Scottish version is the best.

# 9
## All the Fun of the Fare

**Scots may no longer holiday "doon the watter" but they still have a laugh wherever they go.**

DOUGLAS KINNAIRD recalls sunning himself at a hotel's rooftop swimming pool in Spain during siesta time as guests lay in comfortable, soporific silence in the heat.

Suddenly the door burst open as maw, paw, the granny and four weans came in, arms laden with towels, lilos and a bottle of vodka. The shrieking kids barged into the mother who dropped the vodka, shattering the bottle. Another child howled as he cut himself on the glass, the father shouted at the mother for dropping the bottle, the mother shouted at the weans and the granny shouted at the father for shouting.

As the startled guests looked over, Douglas heard one voice declare: "It's Glasgow Fair fortnight."

A SCOTTISH teacher at an international school in Cairo tells us when her class trooped in, and the last pupil left the door open, she automatically asked: "Who was born in a barn?"

Her puzzled Lebanese pupil asked: "Was it Jesus, miss?"

A NORTH Kelvinside reader was in his local where he heard a chap telling his pals about his holiday abroad, adding: "I wouldn't say it was the most money-grabbing budget airline, but the stewardess doing the safety instructions was selling maps showing where the emergency exits were."

FLYING back from Australia, a reader watched the chap in front of her complain when the seat-back televisions were switched off just before landing.

"My movie wasn't finished," he announced.

"I'm sorry sir," said the attendant, "but we need to switch it off during our descent."

"But I don't know how it ends," he continued to wail.

"They all lived happily ever after," announced the attendant as she carried on up the aisle.

AN EDINBURGH reader tells us about the wedding of a local girl to an American. They left to honeymoon in the US, but when they landed at Newark Airport, he went off to the passport queue for American citizens while she stood in the long queue for everyone else.

When she got to the booth and replied that she was on her honey-

moon, the Homeland Security chap looked behind her and asked: "Is it not the custom in your country to take your husband with you?"

AN AGED journalist, who could remember the age of manual type-writers, saw that the ash cloud emanated from Eyjafjallajökull, and told us: "The last time I saw that typed was when I came back to the office drunk and fell asleep on the keyboard."

R&A CAPTAIN Colin Brown was recalling his own sporting past when he spoke at the Trades House of Glasgow.

Colin, in his younger days, turned out for Clydesdale Cricket Club, which once went on tour in Ireland, with the day ending in a dance at which he was whirled around the floor by an enthusiastic Irish girl.

Apologising for his lack of dancing skill, Colin told her: "I'm a little stiff from bowling."

"Oh, I couldn't care less where you're from," she happily told him.

AS WE are always keen to know what our cousins across the Atlantic are thinking, we pass on from a reader in New York State a gag printed in her local newspaper.

A Scot and an American were talking about playing golf during the various seasons of the year. "In most parts of the USA we can't play in the winter time. We have to wait until spring," the American said.

"Why, in Scotland we can even play in the winter. Snow and cold are no object to us," said the Scot.

"Well, what do you do? Paint your balls black?" asked the American.

"No," said the Scot, "we just put on an extra sweater or two."

GORDON DARROCH, who has a keen interest in the poetry of Robert Burns, was telling friends that on a trip to China he found a bookshop that was selling a special Chinese Burns edition. Added Gordon: "I wasn't entirely sure about buying it, but the shopkeeper twisted my arm."

FOSTER EVANS was in a Scottish-themed bar in Florence, and was served the red wine he asked for in an oversized brandy glass.

When he mentioned that this was very generous, and not typically Scottish, the waiter explained that there had been a fight the night before and they were short of unbroken wine glasses.

A PERTH reader who managed to enjoy a holiday in New York in between the ash clouds was much taken with the chap trying to encourage folk to attend a comedy club in Manhattan. He stopped one pregnant young woman and asked her: "Comedy show?"

"No, thanks," she replied.

Not giving up, he then implored, as he pointed at her stomach: "Oh, come on. You might as well make another bad decision."

GLASGOW restaurant owner Alan Mawn was checking in to fly from New York to Glasgow when he noticed that the screen above him was showing the first three letters of everyone's surname. Thus, he and girlfriend Lyndsay Hendrie's names were shown as Maw and Hen.

"Do you think," said an unmistakable Glaswegian accent in the queue behind him, "that Daphne and Paw Broon have been left at hame?"

GERMAN supermarket chain Lidl is becoming popular in Scotland, as shoppers seek out bargains. One Bearsden mother tells us, though, that she had never heard of the chain ten years ago when her young daughter was working in France, and enthusing about how cheap the local Lidl supermarket was.

In particular, she liked its very inexpensive tins of tuna for sandwiches and putting on baked potatoes. It was only weeks later, when shopping with a new French friend, that the young Bearsden girl was asked: "Why are you buying tins of cat food?" She really wished then that she'd paid more attention in her French classes.

A READER in the US sends us a cutting from his local newspaper, which stated: "A Scotsman planning a trip to the Holy Land was aghast when he found it would cost $50 an hour to rent a boat on the Sea of Galilee.

"'Hoots, mon,' he said, 'in Scotland it wouldna ha been more than $20.'

"'That might be true,' said the travel agent, 'but you have to take into account that the Sea of Galilee is water on which our Lord himself walked.'

"'Well, at $50 an hour for a boat,' said the Scotsman, 'it's no wonder he walked'."

DAVID SPEEDIE, working in New York, was in his local shop in Manhattan when an old lady with a shopping cart full of plastic bags and her other worldly goods, joined the queue and muttered to herself that she was sure she was going to win the $200m.

After mentioning this a few times, she was told by the chap next to her that the lottery jackpot that week was $2m. She turned away in disgust with the parting shot: "**** that. I'm not waiting in line for two million!"

JAMES ROBERTSON, in the Alameda County district attorney's office evidence room, tells us: "The Caledonia Club of San Francisco recently held its Highland Games where the Scottish t-shirts on sale included 'Bagpipes – Putting the fun back into funerals'."

STEWART LOTHIAN from Newton Mearns was visiting Vietnam where he bought a bottle of the country's top selling mineral water, La Vie – French for 'life', of course – which was very nice. It was only when he looked at the company's website address on the bottle, laviewater.com, that he felt it might lose its appeal to Glaswegian visitors.

BILL JARDINE in Brittany was visiting Manhattan where a chap was standing on a street corner wearing a placard round his neck which read "Bad advice given – one dollar".

"He was doing a roaring trade," says Bill.

A MILNGAVIE reader on holiday in the US got into conversation with an American woman there with her teenage daughter. The mother was bragging about how bright her daughter was, and how she was going to university to become a lawyer, as she was so smart. It was with comic timing that her daughter interrupted by declaring: "Mom! I've got chewing gum on the camera lens."

A GLASGOW reader back from New York witnessed the legendary New Yorkers' abruptness when he heard a sales lady say to a customer: "Have a nice day," and the retreating, irritated, shopper replied: "I've already made other plans."

AGGRESSIVE New Yorkers, continued. George McDonald of Dowanhill, Glasgow, tells us: "Manhattan beggars and homeless people often suffer the wrath of the locals who tell them, 'Get a job,' or, 'Get a life,' among the more pleasant comments.

"Walking near Central Park, I spotted a beggar holding a large piece of cardboard with rough handwriting – 'Tell me off for a dollar.'"

RAB SPENCE on Skye tells us: "Your story of the guy wearing the sign saying 'Tell me off for a dollar' makes me wonder if it is the same guy my mate saw in New York with a sign around his neck which read: 'Bet you can't hit me with a quarter'.

THE BERLIN WALL anniversary reminded Ronnie Simpson, of Glasgow's Isa Music, of being in East Berlin at the time for a music industry conference. Simple Minds manager Bruce Findlay that night crossed over into West Berlin to check out the music scene.

Heading back to Checkpoint Charlie to cross back east before the curfew, Bruce was met by a chanting crowd of West Germans yelling: "You don't need to go back! You don't need to go back!" So on that historic night, the quote from perhaps one of the first Scots to cross the city divide after the wall was breached was: "Are you kiddin'? My suitcase is back there!"

OUR BERLIN WALL stories remind Dr Tom Smith of being at a medical conference in Berlin in the eighties when a German doctor took him to Checkpoint Charlie. Says Tom: "Directly opposite was a tower with an East German armed guard. Between us and the wall was a fence, then a no-man's-land of bare ground. Directly under the guard, written in green paint on the wall was, 'Celts Furra Cup' and 'Gers Ya Bas'.

"I started laughing. My German friend asked what was so amusing, and I explained. He was dumbfounded.

"'You mean that someone risked his life to write football slogans on this wall, where so many have been shot? This has been on the wall for a year – we had no idea what it meant, or even the language it was in'."

A LANARKSHIRE reader was driving to Newcastle Airport to catch a flight to Greece for his hols when his wife complained about a rattling noise coming from outside the car, and questioning whether the wheels were on tightly enough.

No matter how much he tried to reassure her that wheels don't simply fall off at the wrong time like a clown's car, she insisted that he stop and take a look.

Muttering that they did have a plane to catch, he eventually pulled off the road and went to look at the car on his wife's side. When she wound down the window to ask if he could see anything amiss, he pointed to the belt and buckle of her coat dangling out the side of the shut door.

FAIR MONDAY reminded a Glasgow reader of visiting one of the ruins in Greece where, in an attempt to keep the site tidy, a bin was labelled, first in Greek and then in English, "Empty water bottles".

He watched as a fellow tourist puzzled over the sign, shrugged his shoulders, then poured the contents of his bottle of water into it.

We blame all the airport security malarkey for his confusion.

GLASGOW FAIR continued. An Ayrshire couple on holiday in Portugal e-mailed to tell us that on Fair Monday they were having their nightly stroll, enjoying the buskers and street entertainers. One local was sketching portraits, and as he was studying the face of his next customer, admittedly not the bonniest, an unmistakable Glasgow accent came from the chap standing behind him studying the canvas, who loudly announced: "He's got his work cut out there."

ALSO abroad, but on business, not holidays, was the Wishaw lorry driver who was approached at the queue for the Channel ferry in France by a  character waving a fistful of Euros, offered in return for allowing illegal immigrants to slip aboard his trailer.

Our man told him to beat it, but at that an Irish driver walked up, took the money, and undid the ties on the canvas sides of the truck

next to the Wishaw driver, and the waiting travellers eagerly jumped aboard.

The Irishman then pocketed the money and jumped in the cab of his lorry – which was further down the queue from the one he undid.

A BEARSDEN reader just back from New York was much taken with the conductor on a busy subway who, trying to get commuters to move away from the doors to allow more folk on, announced: "Will all the beautiful, smart people please move up the carriageway, and all the ugly, stupid people remain at the doors?"

ANDY DROUGHT, a research student in Japan, did his bit for cultural understanding by wearing his kilt to a local primary school, where he talked to the pupils about Scotland and even showed them how to dance Strip the Willow.

He was brought back to earth by one of the large number of thank-you letters he received from the pupils in which one youngster wrote: "It was very interesting to see your kilt. It was very kind of you to wear it, as it must have been incredibly embarrassing for you."

A READER holidaying in Spain was lying at the pool beside an extended Scots family when the wife announced to hubby she was going shopping with her mother, and could she have her husband's bank card to extract some euros.

Our reader presumes there was a difficulty in remembering hubby's four-digit pin number, as his mother-in-law returned a few minutes later and unleashed a shrieking scream so rarely heard at a Spanish swimming pool: "Paul, when did Thistle win the League Cup?"

READER David Gray recalls being a student in Gateshead where, after a trip to Greece, he went to Tesco to buy the ingredients for moussaka. When he asked an assistant if they had aubergines she discussed this with other staff before telling him: "Nah, only Levi's and Wrangler's."

A PARTICK reader on holiday in Wales tells us he visited the local cinema where the glass-fronted message board outside said the film that evening was on at 6.59. When he bought his ticket he commented on the time being very exact. "We've lost our number 7," the ticket-seller explained.

ENJOYING the good weather on Rothesay was a big family group, when the mother suddenly shrieked that she had lost sight of their five-year-old son.

A reader gives full marks for trying to the lady's husband, who attempted, but failed, to calm her down by telling her: "Don't worry. It's an island. He can't get off."

READER Fred Gibbons was visiting Arran when he walked towards a family arguing near the Brodick ferry terminal. The mother had walked on towards Fred while her husband and daughter hung back, with the daughter cartoonishly climbing on to the railing to pretend throwing herself in the sea while her dad, playing along, restrained her.

Seeing the woman wasn't watching, Fred told her as they passed: "Don't look now, but your daughter is trying to throw herself off the bridge."

"Only in my dreams," the woman replied, without a backward glance.

INEVITABLY, we have to end the Glasgow holiday fortnight stories with the classic, i.e. very old, gag of the Glasgow chap applying for a job as a bus driver where he was asked questions about how he would deal with drunks or rowdy passengers. He was doing well until he was asked: "What would you do if you can't get the fare?" Yes, altogether now: "I'd just take the first two weeks in August."

# 10
# Carbon Dating

**Seemingly, getting old is a laughing matter.**

A GRANDFATHER visiting his family in Newton Mearns watched as his grandson put on elbow pads, knee pads and a helmet before announcing: "I'm going to ride my bike, grand-da."

"Where?" asked the puzzled old fella. "Through a mine-field?"

WE ARE told about the little boy visiting his granny who asked her, as his granddad had died many years ago, whether she was going to get a new boyfriend.

"This is my boyfriend now," his granny told him, pointing to her old telly in the corner, which was permanently on.

Imagine his parents' consternation though when he went home, and casually mentioned: "Granny was banging her boyfriend this afternoon."

JOHN DAVIS in Greenock overhears some mature ladies discussing a dating agency one had joined, but she was complaining that the chaps on it were a bit elderly. "They should rename it," she told her pals, "the Carbon Dating Agency."

READER Jim Quinn passed a smartly dressed elderly couple near the Hilton Hotel in Glasgow's west end and overheard the lady say to the man: "The next time I wear this outfit could be your funeral."

"Who said romance was dead?" says Jim.

A RETIRED gent in Ayr was telling his pals that west of Scotland travel agents were cancelling trips to Lourdes and redirecting folk to Ayr, where miracles were happening every day.

When his pals looked quizzical, he added: "Have you seen all those folk parking in the disabled bays in the High Street with their blue badges on the dashboard, then sprinting across the road to the shops?"

ALAN BARLOW was in a Largs pub when an elderly customer, bent over and using a walking stick, came in and was asked if he was a pensioner.

"Naw, son," he replied. "I'm frae Greenock, and I'm just wore oot."

A READER attending her pensioner's club in her local community centre was proudly shown a bluebird that a fellow pensioner had just had tattooed on her shoulder. Our surprised reader asked why she had waited until she was seventy to have a tattoo.

"Until now," she replied, "I was afraid of what my mother would say."

A BISHOPBRIGGS mother tells us about taking her young son to visit his grandmother whose budgie had just died. Seeing her son staring at the empty cage she gently explained that the budgie had gone to heaven.

"Why didn't he take his cage with him?" her son asked.

A READER holidaying in America heard an elderly Scottish couple in front of him registering at a hotel. They were told their room had twin beds, and asked if that was a problem.

"I don't know. We've been sharing the same bed for over thirty years," the husband replied.

Our reader thought that was so romantic until the wife piped up: "If he snores, how can I reach over and punch him when we're in separate beds?"


A RENFREWSHIRE reader in his fifties had the shock realisation that he must be getting old when he took the change out of his pocket to pay for some messages, and after he hesitated for a second, the assistant reached across and went through the coins in his palm for the correct money.


A GLASGOW reader was in a West-End bar where he spotted a chap of a certain age, who should have known better, chatting up a woman many years younger than him.

His patter didn't appear to be working, as our reader heard the young woman rather viciously, but perhaps not unfairly, ask the chap: "Are you really that bald, or is your neck just blowing a bubble?"


THE GOOD weather bringing out the gardeners reminded Donald Grant in Paisley of when a colleague retired to a cottage near Dunoon and planted trees and bushes around his garden, leaving the labels on to help identify them. Next morning, when he looked out, he saw that rabbits or deer had eaten all the leaves and tender branches. "Perhaps they thought I'd left a menu for them," he later told pals.

A READER attending the 100th birthday party of a friend's great grandmother asked the old lady if she was now looking forward to her 101st birthday.

"Yes," replied the birthday girl. "I'm encouraged by the statistic that very few people in Scotland die between their 100th and 101st birthdays."

LATEST figures from TV Licensing show that there are still more than 500 folk in Glasgow with a black-and-white television licence as opposed to the more expensive colour one. In Edinburgh, the figure is a mere 200.

Good to see so many folk keeping the old sets going – we would never suggest they are on the fiddle.

It does, though, remind us of the time Lanarkshire MP Frank Roy, at a pensioners' rally, asked those over seventy-five to stand up. After much scraping of chairs and zimmers, they dutifully got to their feet, when Frank then declared: "All the rest of you have a good look at them. Now that they get a free TV licence they can buy the next round at the bar."

A READER waiting at his optician in Glasgow's city centre the other day watched an old chap sitting opposite gesture at the glossy magazines on the table in front of him and tell his wife: "If we could read them, we wouldn't have to be here, would we?"

MARION CAMPBELL in Bishopbriggs was looking after her four-year-old grandson who continually said "What?" to every question, so like every good granny she told him: "You don't say 'what' you say 'pardon.'"

All seemed well until the lad spotted a telephone engineer working outside and asked: "Pardon is that man doing up that pole?"

# 11
# Aff His Lead

**Just in case you were wondering why there is a kitten on the cover . . .**

A READER tells us she brought home a kitten for the family, even though her husband didn't seem too keen. As he sat reading his newspaper, she was flicking a piece of paper on the floor for the kitten to chase, and then happily declared: "We should get him a ball of wool."

"What, can he knit as well?" came the bored voice from behind the paper.

A MILNGAVIE reader had booked a mobile pet-groomer to give her dog a clipping for the summer. Her husband walked in and declared: "Twenty-five quid? I get my hair cut for less than half that."

The pet-groomer merely replied: "Yes, but I am assuming you don't bite."

MISSING the point was the chap in the park who didn't clean up after his dog. When an irate fellow park user pointed out the sign stating "Dog fouling. Maximum fine £100", he replied: "Nothing for me to worry about. My dog doesn't play football."

A CHAP in Newton Mearns had obviously taken his brave pills when he went with his wife to a cat rescue centre to choose a family pet. After picking up a variety of cats of all different shapes and colours, she held two in her arms, and asked him which he preferred.

"The striped one makes you look thinner," he couldn't help himself saying.

WE HEAR from Greenock where a chap with a criminal record was being interviewed by police after CCTV pictures suggested he had been involved in a robbery. He was denying even owning the distinctive hat being worn by the robber when his dog trotted into the room and dropped said hat in front of him.

"Look at that," said one of the cops. "Even yer dug has grassed you up."

A READER tells us the chap in the pub was complaining about his neighbour's dog constantly barking in the garden and driving everyone mad. "I'm going to kidnap the dog," the chap declared, "and put it in my garden to see how he likes it."

AN EDINBURGH reader tells us of her embarrassment on an American ranch holiday when she was asked if she would prefer a western or an English saddle. She asked what the difference was and was told the western had a horn. Without thinking she replied: "Are we going out into traffic?" before realising the horn was merely a hump on the saddle.

READER Donald Macdonald tells us about the uniquely Glaswegian words of encouragement as the cyclists on the Pedal for Scotland charity run from Glasgow to Edinburgh were going through Easterhouse. One chap with a large alsatian shouted: "If youse get tired oan the next hill, I'll let him aff his lead."

CLIMATE change was being discussed in a Motherwell pub the other day where a regular opined: "They say that if the planet keeps on warming up, the only place where you will be able to see a polar bear is in a zoo.

"So," he added, "no change there for us then."

"BEFORE they invented the Internet," declared the chap in the pub, "women must have spent a lot of time wondering what to do with all their pictures of cats."

WE ARE told about a distraught dog owner who took her pet to the vet because of an unusual growth in the poor mutt's mouth. After examining it, the vet asked the owner if she had any children.

"Oh, my god! Is it contagious?" she shouted.

"No," the bemused vet replied. "It's bubblegum."

NEWS from Central America, where a number of newspapers carried the headline: "Chinchilla becomes Costa Rica President". This, of course, was a reference to politician Laura Chinchilla, and not the furry rodent.

Nonetheless, a number of weary British voters have already declared that a hamster in a wheel couldn't be any worse than Gordon Brown.

A READER back from holiday in Texas swears blind that the preacher in the church he attended used the prayer: "Lord, help me to be the person my dog thinks I am."

A MILNGAVIE reader back from a safari in the Masai Mara national park in Kenya tells us a fellow safari goer was ticked off by the guide for reading her guidebook during the safari as the guide didn't want her to miss any sightings. He thought the guide was very clever in telling her: "Don't try to read between the lions."

THERE is the daft joke about the minister who lost his bible when out for a walk, and couldn't find it. He prayed for its safe return, and two days later, a dog came to his door with the bible in its mouth.

"It's a miracle!" shouted the delighted minister.

"Not really," replied the dog. "Your name was written inside the cover."

# 12
## Ram-Raiding the Co-op

JIM FRASER from Elie was in Anstruther behind a fisherman's wife who was paying her gas and electricity bills, and he heard her commenting on how expensive the utilities had become. As the woman put it: "They're just like fishermen – if you dinna watch them, they're no long in gettin' on top o' you."

EDDIE McFADDEN was chatting to a woman in the East End of Glasgow who was the last remaining tenant in a dilapidated tenement block. She cheerfully remarked that in order to be re-housed the landlord would have to "give her condensation".

"Looking around the flat," said Eddie, "it appeared to me that the council had already upheld their end of the bargain."

THE SUNNY weather brought out the first of the year's barbecues. But one young Glasgow chap moved his barbecue indoors when it turned chilly. Unfortunately, the smoke filled his flat, much to his guests' alarm.

One young girl, the daughter of a firefighter, knew what to do, and shouted at the party-giver to fetch a damp tea towel.

He dashed back from the kitchen with one – and then stood wringing it out over the barbecue.

AYRSHIRE councillor John Reid tells us that a van parked in Cumnock's Main Street the other day did not have its handbrake properly applied, and, with no one in it, gradually rolled down the hill and smashed into the Co-op funeral parlour's window.

A passer-by looked at the van embedded in the smashed window and declared: "Only in Cumnock would someone try to ram-raid the funeral parlour."

NORMAN McLEAN in Ayr tells us about a group of architectural students from Glasgow who were on a field trip to York where they stayed in the local university's halls of residence.

Invited to a university dinner, one student was perhaps overawed when he was asked by an academic further up the table: "Which course are you on?"

His startled reply of "the soup" will haunt him forever.

IT IS sad to report that some folk can be less than sympathetic to street mendicants. An Edinburgh reader saw a chap, emerging unsteadily from a New Town wine bar, being asked by a poor soul sitting cross-legged on a blanket in the street: "Any change?"

The toper replied: "Nope. Still got a big house and a fast car," and walked past him.

"WHEN I was young," said the pub philosopher, "I had an imaginary friend.

"Now that I'm on Facebook, I have 260 of them."

MARTIN STEEL in Hamilton bought an engagement card on which was printed on the back "Not suitable for children under thirty-six months" and he worried that we're setting the age limit far too low.

THE GEEKS amongst us have been debating whether Apple's new gizmo, the iPad, is worth having.

We're not sure how politically correct the young suit in the bar was when he declared: "Having an iPad is like having a blonde model for a girlfriend.

"Awesome to look at and tell your mates about, but useless at everything else."

THE WORTH of punctuation was brought home to Neil Smith at the Royal Navy's Devonport docks where someone had put a hand-written sign at the shower block stating: "Do not enter female in shower."

He really felt a full-stop in the middle would have avoided any misunderstandings.

AS ITHERS see us . . . A reader in Texas sends us this from his local newspaper: "An atheist was fishing, when suddenly his boat was attacked by the Loch Ness monster. The beast tossed him and his boat high into the air, then opened its mouth to swallow him. The man cried out, 'Oh, God! Help me!'

"At once, the ferocious attack froze, and as the atheist hung in mid-air, a booming voice came down, 'I thought you didn't believe in Me?'

"'Come on, God, give me a break!' the man pleaded. 'Two minutes ago, I didn't believe in the Loch Ness monster either!'"

NIGEL ROBSON spots a Christmas poster outside a kirk in Greenbank, Edinburgh, which reads: "Carpenter from Nazareth needs joiners".

DOUG KING recalls an old colleague whose secretary brought him a letter to sign. Sadly, she had, by mistake, typed the town of Biggar as Buggar. He attached a note stating "Make Buggar Biggar" and passed it back. Of course, inevitably, the redraft came back with Buggar in a larger type.

DAVID WILL in Milngavie tells us that when the Christmas lights were switched on in the Ayrshire hamlet of Kilbirnie, Santa stepped off the Irn-Bru bus, and told the assembled crowd: "It's great to be back in Kilbirnie – I love Kilbirnie."

"You don't get out much then, Santa," shouted back a local worthy.

A BISHOPBRIGGS reader tells us he was advising his regular insurance agent that he could find car insurance a lot cheaper on the

Internet. "Ah, yes," his agent told him. "But if you were in an accident, who do you want to help you: a man or a mouse?"

A READER attending a wine-tasting in Glasgow was told by the wine-seller: "Do you know what the most popular wine is at Christmas?"
    When he replied in the negative, he was told: "There's never anything good on the telly."

THE DIFFERENCE between Glasgow and Edinburgh was summed up for a reader who moved to Edinburgh from Glasgow, and shortly afterwards was chatting to her new neighbour over the garden fence. Eventually the neighbour suggested: "Would you like to come round for coffee?"

"That would be nice," said our lady from Glasgow, who was about to gather up her children for the visit.

"How about a week on Thursday?" the Edinburgh lady continued.

AFTER the story about the treasure hunter in Stirling finding the hoard of Iron Age gold jewellery, a Corstorphine reader tells us his pal was inspired by the find, took a new metal detector to the beach and had enthusiastically dug down six feet before he realised he was wearing steel toecaps.

AYR ARTIST Sandra Ratcliffe, en route to Gigha for an exhibition of her paintings, was stuck in the lift of her block of flats with many of her canvasses.

She shouted for help, and neighbours called the fire brigade.

The firefighter who prised the lift doors open, looked at all the paintings surrounding her, and remarked: "Just how long have you been in here?"

A KILMAURS reader hopes the customer in front of him at the check-out at Marks & Spencer was joking when she was offered a gent's tie for only a penny by the check-out assistant. It was part of a promotion by the store to mark its 125th anniversary.

The woman took the tie and told the assistant: "It'll do for his Christmas while I'm away on my Caribbean cruise."

AN E-MAIL user had to contact all his friends to tell them his e-mail address had been hijacked by a virus, and that they should treat all his future e-mails as spam.

"I'm sure I can speak for everyone," a pal cruelly e-mailed back, "when I say that we were already doing that with your stuff."

A TELEVISION insider sends us a letter received by ITV. It reads: "After much soul-searching, I regret to inform you that I wish to take no further part in *I'm A Celebrity . . . Get Me Out of Here!*

"Although initially happy with the amount of air time I received, I began to realise the public must hate me, as I was picked to appear in every bush tucker trial.

"This has been a real ordeal for me, especially as I have now been bitten by a number of hideous creatures, and I can't take it any more.

"Yours sincerely, Charlie the Cockroach."

"CHRISTMAS wouldn't be Christmas without M&S", according to the latest advertisement. "Quite correct," points out a young reader. "Otherwise it would be Chrita."

A YOUNG philanthropist in Bishopbriggs was watching a charity's television appeal, and was so moved, she phoned to sponsor a child in Africa.

Due to other charitable donations, she explained she only wanted to commit to £5 a month instead of the £10 requested in the advert.

The Glasgow call centre worker argued: "So you would only like to sponsor half a child – so your child's only gonna have the wan shoe then?"

Not to be bullied, she told him: "Well I'll be able to pick him out in the next advert then."

DONALD MACASKILL was visiting the stunning Glasgow Boys art exhibition at Kelvingrove, which includes a number of garden paintings with rows of cabbages.

As he studied George Henry's "A Cottar's Garden", a fellow visitor told her companion: "'En plein air' just means that the artists painted outside instead of in the studio."

"I'm not surprised," remarked her companion, "if they ate all those cabbages."

COLIN WALKER in Hamilton confesses that he thought he was being awfully smart when he was a student in Glasgow, and a street mendicant, with outstretched hand, asked: "Somethin' furra cup o' tea, pal?"

So Colin handed him the two sugar sachets he had purloined from the Students Union.

Adds Colin: "Naturally, I was thanked in the usual Glasgow fashion by being told to go and take a running jump to myself."

OUR TALES of street mendicants remind Jim Hair in Dalry of watching a chap who, after being asked, "Any chance of 10p for a cup of tea?" by a beggar, reached into his pocket for a coin, and told him: "Here's 20p – get me one as well."

THOMAS MILLS tells us he was walking through Queen Street Station when a vagrant asked him for change for his train fare home. Thomas told him he didn't have any money and walked on.

Minutes later, Thomas was standing in the nearby Sammy Dow's pub when the beggar came in, put a huge pile of coins on the bar and asked the barman to change it for notes. Then, spotting Thomas eyeing him from further up the bar, the chap turned and told him: "Well, you lied anaw!"

NEWS that the Woodside Social Club in Glasgow's west end is being converted into flats reminds Susan Young of when she first moved into the West End and heard about the club, which has a well-used pool hall upstairs.

Unfortunately, Susan misunderstood what was meant by the "Woodside pool hall" and eagerly turned up one day with her swimming costume and towel, which, of course, got her some funny looks from the local lads carrying snooker cues.

A GLASGOW chap, obviously wanting to confirm stereotypes, tells us about being out with his blonde girlfriend who needed a cash machine. He told her the corner shop had one, but it was the kind that charged you three quid to make a withdrawal.

"That's OK," she told him, before taking out three £1 coins and trying to push them in the tiny slot where your bank card goes.

BUT SHE'S not alone. Janice Carter's husband once repaired photo booths, and she tells us: "One call-out was for the coin slot being blocked, and often this was as a result of ne'er-do-wells inserting scrap paper in the coin slots. Not this time – someone had tried to pay for their £3 photo with three pound notes."

READER Jess Dalrymple was in a small Gallowgate takeaway shop when an expansive chap came in and cheerily asked the young woman serving: "What's good for eating the day?"

"McDonald's," the bored teenager replied.

"Aye, Ah'll dae that then," the chap replied, and walked out the door.

JIM DELAHUNT in Ardrossan says the tale is told locally of the minister who regularly was shaved by the local barber, who was a member of his flock.

Says Jim: "Unfortunately, the barber had the previous evening imbibed rather too well of the juice of the barley and despite concentrating, his trembling hand caused him to nick the minister's cheek and draw blood.

"'That's the whisky that causes that,' said the minister solemnly.

"'That's right,' replied the barber. 'It does make your skin a hell of a tender.'"

A WAITER on the south side of Glasgow said he managed to bite his tongue when a customer who had a glass of Coke that she had drunk waved him over. "There's only melted ice left," she said, holding up the glass. "I don't like it."

Asked if she would like something else, she replied: "Just a glass of water."

# 13
## Start Spreading the News

Even in these frightening days of redundancies throughout the country to pay for the greedy bankers, the workers can still raise a smile.

N forms: a North Kelvinside reader tells us
ced, when he reached the box which asked "Salary
te in it "Friday".

PAT ELLEW in London once worked in the Clyde shipyards, where a notorious barber in Port Glasgow was known as "Sweeney" Boyle because of his carefree style.

Says Pat: "He was giving a guy a shave, and, true to form, he kept nicking the guy's neck, who told him, 'Ho! Be careful!'

"Eventually, he cuts the guy seriously enough to draw blood. 'Huv ye goat anither razor?' the guy finally shouts out.

"Sweeney, imperturbable as ever, asks him why he wants another razor, and the customer replies, 'Ah want tae defend masel'."

AT THE annual dinner of the Bonnetmakers and Dyers Trade at Glasgow's Trades House, speaker Neil McIntosh spotted a fellow vet in the audience and explained: "We have something in common. When we were both in our teens, we aspired to being a lawyer or an accountant.

"Unfortunately, we did far too well in our Higher exams."

DEBBIE MEEHAN tells us of a friend having her nails manicured who was asked by the beautician what she did for a living.

"I'm an anaesthetist," she replied.

"What's that?" said the beautician.

"I put people to sleep," she explained in simple terms.

"Oh, is that not very sad?" said the girl.

WE FELT for the guy in the West-End bar who was asked by a comely young woman: "You look really familiar – what do you do?"

"I'm an actor and a musician," he modestly told her.

She stared at him a bit longer before adding: "No, that's not it. Do you work in Sainsbury's?"

"Well, that as well . . ." he muttered.


AN EDINBURGH reader claims a puzzled colleague looked at the fire blanket on the wall in their company's kitchen and asked: "Why would anyone feel cold if the building was on fire?"

A READER who handed in her notice from her job when she became pregnant had to go through one of these exit interviews – the latest piece of pointless form-filling dreamed up by corporate human resource departments.

When she got to the question, "Could any action have been taken to prevent you from leaving?" she merely wrote down: "Birth control."

UBIQUITOUS in the streets and closes of Glasgow are the red rubber bands that postmen use. Postie Kirsty Lees tells us that a colleague was asked by a youth in the street: "Huv ye any spare elastics?"

The postman handed over a few of the rubber bands, then walked on. Seconds later, one of them pinged off the back of his neck as the youngster scooted off laughing.

OUR ADMIRATION for newspaper street vendors grows with the story in the book *Century Bhoys*, a history of Celtic's greatest goal-scorers, about early Celtic player Sandy McMahon, who scored 177 times in the 1890s. Authors Paul Cuddihy and David Friel relate that when the former president of France, Patrice de Mac-Mahon, Duc de Magenta, died in 1893, enterprising newspaper sellers in Glasgow tried to boost sales by shouting, "McMahon deid! McMahon deid!"

OUR ADMIRATION of newspaper street vendors reminds Alec Findlay in Kilmarnock of the newspaper seller in Glasgow's Central Station on the day that Frank Sinatra died. The chap was shouting "Frank Sinatra died!" and then broke into a chorus of "Start spreading the news . . ."

GLEN ELLIOT in Elgin tells us of when John Brown's was taken over by French company UiE. Glen was at a contracts meeting when it was proposed an order be given to a company in England, but a colleague argued: "The last time we gave them a big order they took us to the cleaners."

Says Glen: "The French project manager thought it was about time he made an impact on the proceedings and declared in broken English, 'I've never been to the Cleaners. Please arrange a visit for me.'"

OUR TALES of barbers remind Joe Boyle in Kings Park of the classic – i.e. old – yarn of the Royal Navy rating from Glasgow on shore leave in Malta getting a haircut where he found himself in the chair next to an admiral.

Says Joe: "When the barber dealing with the admiral inquired if 'Sir would like any pomade on his hair?' the admiral replied, laughing, 'No, thanks, my wife would think I had been in a brothel.'

"When the same question was asked of the matelot a few seconds later, he replied, 'Aye, on ye go, son. My wife's never been in a brothel.'"

"I WAS sent to an anger management course," said the chap in the pub the other night. "It's all the rage."

A STORY about counterfeit goods reminds Gordon Liddle of being on shore-leave in Singapore where he bought an album by The Police. He realised it was counterfeit when he noticed that the track "Walking on the Moon" was printed on the cover as "Wailing on the Moon". After his shipmates listened to it a few times, they felt it was more than appropriate.

READER Margaret Wright in Glasgow tells us about her driving instructor husband taking a foreign student out on a Sunday. The pupil asked at the end of the lesson if he knew where he could find a bookie.

Her husband's chatty reply that he didn't think they were open on a Sunday, and that his student didn't look like someone who gambled, brought a puzzled look and the reply: "It's Valentine's Day. I need to get my wife a bouquet."

A READER tells us the company he works for has recently changed the bank it deals with, and a meeting was held on the premises with the new bankers.

They were asked if they wanted a tour of the factory, and one of the bankers asked if it was safe.

"No, you don't need safety glasses," he was told.

"I meant from the workers," the banker replied.

"WHY IS it," asked the chap in the pub, "that the blokes who wear Bluetooth headsets in the street look like the sort of people nobody would want to phone?"

THE RASH of redundancies has left a number of husbands temporarily at home doing the domestic chores while their wives are out working. Some though, take longer than others, to get a grasp of it all.

As one such house-husband explained to his mates: "The wife came home and asked if I'd remembered to put a wash on.

"When I said 'yes' she asked if I'd remembered to separate the whites from the coloured clothes.

"Apparently telling her, 'Yes, I put the coloured stuff at the bottom and the whites on top' was not the right answer."

THE RE-OPENING of an Islay distillery to safeguard future supplies reminds reader Jim Morrison of a dockers' strike in Aberdeen some years ago that was disrupting supplies of goods to Shetland. Jim was then on an oil tanker, and when they picked up the pilot at Lerwick, his captain asked the pilot: "How are things in Lerwick? Any shortages?"

The pilot replied: "Well, there was a rumour last night about a pending shortage of whisky, which caused a bit of panic drinking, but apart from that everything is OK."

DURING the cold winter, a reader reminded us of the employee who arrived an hour late for work one winter's morning and explained to his boss that it was so slippery outside that for every step forward he took, he slipped two back.

"Is that so?" replied his suspicious boss. "Then how did you ever get here?"

"I gave up and started for home," replied the tardy worker.

THE NEWS story about a translator being sought to make Glaswegians easier to understand reminds Gerry Burke of a pay discussion at John Brown's yard on the Clyde when a shop steward declared: "Ah've tellt ye ... nae mair moolah, the bears are oot!"

An American executive turned to a local colleague for elucidation, only to be told: "Basically, he's sayin' the ba's on the slates."

A READER tells us he got a bit disoriented in a large Glasgow store and had to ask a dour-looking security guard where the exit was. "Are you trying to get out of here?" the chap asked.

When our reader answered in the affirmative, the security guard pointed towards the exit and told him: "So am I."

A GLASGOW letting agent tells us someone finally gave her the answer she's been waiting for. When someone phones seeking to rent a property, she runs through some set questions, which includes "Children?"

"Yes, two, aged nine and twelve," the caller replied.

"Animals?" she asked.

"No," she replied. "Both well behaved."

ONE OF Scotland's leading businessmen, Sir Tom Hunter, was giving an overview of the past year in business at the Entrepreneurial Exchange's annual awards ceremony.

We don't think he was being entirely serious when he proclaimed: "I'd also like to thank lawyers and accountants for pointing out the bleeding obvious, what I already knew, and then charging me handsomely for it."

# 14
# Clatty Dumpling

**Of course, we're very friendly to tourists – but they do make us smile.**

NORMAN BROWN in Barassie wonders if the foreign chap at Glasgow's Buchanan Bus Station ever reached his destination when he approached the driver of a parked bus and politely asked if it was going to Ayr. The driver shook his head, pointed to the bus at the next stand, and told him: "Naw, pal. Err Err Err."

AN AMERICAN couple tell us they arrived for a holiday in Scotland, but their luggage didn't. Assured it would be delivered to their Glasgow hotel later, they headed off, stopping at a chemist's for some toiletries. Clutching only their plastic bags from Boots, they checked into the hotel where the receptionist told them: "Ah, matching luggage I see."

IT'S GREAT to see the paddle steamer Waverley back cruising on the Clyde. Waverley fan Ian Bruce overheard an American tourist on board saying: "I just love the crew's quaint Gaelic accent."

Says Ian: "We didn't have the heart to tell her they were Polish."

OUR MENTION of the paddle steamer Waverley reminds a colleague of the time the late photographer Jack Middleton sailed on it to Arran where, in need of solid sustenance, he asked two local ladies where he might find a curry shop. They indicated a building 300 yards away where Jack was eventually seen cursing the two women as he stood outside . . . Curry's, the newsagent.

JOHN PARK in Motherwell watched a couple of foreign visitors ask a local where they could get a pub lunch. When he pointed out two pubs that served food, the visitors asked him which was the best.

John heard the chap reply: "Let me put it to you this way. Whichever one of the two you go to, you'll wish you had gone to the other one."

A READER in Inveraray tells us about a couple of English tourists who looked at the old-fashioned "Apothecary" sign over the chemist's shop, with one turning to the other and asking: "I don't know any Gaelic. I wonder what it means?"

AN AMERICAN student in Glasgow tells us that before coming to study here she asked a Glaswegian attending her American

college what local customs and phrases she should learn. The Glasgow
chap declined to tell her, adding: "That would just deprive the locals in
Glasgow of your comedic value if I told you."

A BISHOPBRIGGS reader on a visit to Dublin overheard an American pointing to the menu board outside a pub and telling his wife: "Guinness stew? I thought they only made beer."

JAY SMART heard an American tourist in Glasgow's venerable Babbity Bowster trying to order the clootie dumpling from the traditional Scottish menu, but it came out as "the clatty dumpling".

Unless of course, mused Jay, he really had picked up the local lingo.

AN AMERICAN website gives details of which airports are good to sleep in if you have to wait overnight for a flight.

The Scottish airports are generally well reviewed except by a chap called John who perhaps didn't quite get the local accent, as he wrote about Glasgow Airport: "It wouldn't have been that bad, except they decided to test the fire alarm and every single smoke alarm in the entire building.

"The last straw was when I asked the worker how much longer they were going to be testing, and he mumbled something in an unintelligible dialect which I swear didn't really exist – he was probably just messing with me."

THE REFURBISHED five-star Turnberry Hotel planned to name a £700-a-night luxury suite after whoever won the Open there. Thus it was named the Cink Suite.

We can't help wondering though about the confusion during telephone bookings when customers reply: "At that price that's the least I expect."

STEWARTON businessman Robert Miller is such a fan of Lamlash Golf Club on Arran that some years ago on his birthday he helped provide a drinking fountain halfway round the course, which was inaugurated with some whisky poured over it.

Back at the club on his 85th birthday, he jokingly rededicated the fountain by again pouring some whisky over it.

Just after, some visiting Canadians playing the course took a drink at the fountain and then told Robert, who was still sitting there, that they had fallen so much in love with Scotland that they would swear that even the drinking water was beginning to taste like whisky.


AN EDINBURGH reader swears blind that a bus-load of American tourists was emptying in the centre of Edinburgh, and one of them stared at the craters in the road caused by the work on the new tramline. "Was this terrorism?" he asked a local.

"Aye," he was told, "but round here we call them councillors."

# 15
## The Papped Oot Fairy

**Every Glaswegian wants to be a performer. But here are some stories of the real thing.**

READER John Boyd tells us that at the *Aladdin* panto at the King's in Glasgow, actor Gerard Kelly as Aladdin asked the audience if he should trust the baddie, and of course the whole theatre shouted back: "No!"

Later, when Aladdin was locked in the cave, the silence was broken by a lone Glasgow voice shouting: "Well, we telt ye."

COMEDIAN Paul Merton's return to do improv at the Glasgow Comedy Festival reminded a reader of Paul's last improv outing in Glasgow when he asked the audience to "name an item in the kitchen".

"The wife," shouted back one brave Glaswegian.

SOLDIER BLUE singer Buffy Sainte-Marie was a highlight of the Celtic Connections festival in Glasgow.

It reminds us of when Buffy, a Cree Native American, Ramblin' Jack Elliott, billed as "America's Roving Cowboy", and Blind Gary Davis, the black blues great, flew in to Glasgow for a folk festival some years ago.

Scottish folk luminaries Josh Macrae and Hamish Imlach were sent to collect them and, having a swift drink or two beforehand, Hamish pointed out he had only seen their faces on old album covers and asked Josh: "How will we recognise them?"

Josh replied: "A blind black man, a Cree Indian and a cowboy? If we don't recognise them, Hamish, I'm giving up the drink."

COMEDIAN Bill Bailey held up a lute-like instrument at his concert at Glasgow's Theatre Royal and asked the audience what it was.

After a few wrong guesses, a woman shouted out: "It's an oud!"

Clearly impressed by the wisdom of Glaswegians, Bill asked how she knew.

The wee Glasgow wifey shouted back: "Ma pal was here last night, and she told me!"

EDDIE McFADDEN was at The Ferry gig of Glasgow prog rockers Abel Ganz when a band member announced that the next track was from their new album *Shooting Albatross*. A confused punter in the crowd shouted out: "Who's Albert Ross?"

A READER watching a street performer in Glasgow's city centre was impressed by the performer's cheek when he shouted at a couple leaving before he had finished his act: "Hey! I didn't leave when you got here."

A HAMILTON reader watched a performer in Aberdeen who enthralled his audience by juggling lit torches. She adds: "Everyone was watching in awe at a safe distance when a jaikie broke the circle and went right up to him, fag in mouth, and asked the immortal line, 'Huv ye got a light, son?'"

OUR MENTION of the late lamented folk singer Danny Kyle's challenging humour reminds Rab Spense on Skye of Danny compéring a concert in Londonderry in the seventies. Danny bounded on to the stage, which had a backdrop of the Londonderry coat of arms that depicts a skeleton.

Says Rab: "Danny walked to centre stage and, pointing over his shoulder, said, 'Whit's that? A Catholic waitin' fur a hoose?' Till his dying day, he didn't know how he got out alive."

GLASGOW Comedy Festival performer Vladimir McTavish tells us some expatriates in Kuwait, denied pork products, asked if he could smuggle them in some pork pies when he was going out for a gig. "Getting six pork pies in a condom up your backside is no joke," he adds.

READER Jim McCrudden was leaving the Dublin show of comedian Michael McIntyre when he heard a fellow attender say to his mate: "It really is the best medicine, isn't it?"

"What, laughter?" asked his pal.

"No, alcohol," the chap replied.


DAVID MACLEOD was watching an outdoor magician in Glasgow's Buchanan Street who was being heckled by youths. Eventually he asked: "So, where are you boys from?"

"Alloa," said one.

"Great place to come from," said the magician, who added: "God-awful place to have to go back to though."


AND JIM SCOTT in Midlothian was in Glasgow's Buchanan Street when the street magician discovered that the audience member helping him was newly divorced. "I've had two unhappy marriages," the entertainer announced. "My first wife left me.

"And the second one won't."


A READER was at the *Pinocchio* panto at the Pavilion when the fire alarm rang during the performance. The 1,200 audience members dutifully trooped out into the street. They were followed out by the cast in their costumes, which led to one wee Glesga wummin saying to her tot: "Look, hen, Ah told you it wis real – even the fairy got papped oot!"


TO SEE oursels as ithers see us . . . one of the acts at Slumdog restaurant's comedy nights observed: "I used to think that Irn-Bru was just a drink until I came to Glasgow and realised the young women here think it's a shade."

WHEN the Edinburgh Festival began, it was surely wrong of the Glaswegian who asked us: "How do you get an actor away from your door?" He then added the answer: "Pay him for the pizza."

SINGER songwriter Paul Carrack, like many of his audience at Glasgow's Concert Hall, is not in his first flush of youth. So, many could sympathise when Paul sang the Marvin Gaye hit 'What's Going On', and when he got to the line "Who are they to judge us simply because our hair is long?" he actually intoned: "Simply because our hair is gone?"

EVER-SMILING, buck-toothed television presenter Alan Carr was commemorated in Mark Borkowski's exhibition of memorable Fringe publicity stunts, Twithibition.

It recalls Carr performing at an Edinburgh old people's home and being rewarded with a crowd, which, having just eaten lunch, was falling asleep and snoring loudly throughout his set. One man kept on laughing hysterically – only stopping for the punch lines.

The headline that launched Carr's career was – "Young comedian dies in Edinburgh nursing home."

So, not much changed in Carr's career, then, say the ungenerous.

THE TOURING stage show of *Strictly Come Dancing* was on at Glasgow's SECC on Valentine's Day, and among the mainly female audience were a few partners who had been dragged along. In the gents' toilet afterwards, a *Herald* reader heard one chap at the urinals announce with a sigh: "That's it over, then."

The chap next to him added: "Ah, well, it keeps her happy."

But the more pessimistic chap next to them added: "It will be *Dancing on Ice* next."

COMEDY sketch artists Chris Forbes, Kevin Mains and James Kirk were rehearsing at Glasgow's Panopticon Music Hall in Trongate, one of the world's oldest music halls, when they were told it was haunted by ghosts who didn't like any technology. Film crews, for example, had found their cameras inexplicably not working.

Says Chris: "We were using a laser pen for one sketch, and it stopped working. The battery had gone dead, so James went out to buy one. While he was away though, we found one and replaced it.

"When James came back, we insisted that before we change the battery, we get in a circle and ask the ghosts to please let us use the laser pen, and that we hoped they didn't mind us being there. When James tried the pen and it worked, he almost soiled himself."

AMERICAN singer songwriter Steve Earle gave his Glasgow audience a brief language lesson, while tuning up for one song. "Mandolin," he explained, "that's Italian for out of tune."

A LENZIE reader watched a street performer in Glasgow's Buchanan Street who asked a volunteer: "Is this your girlfriend?" while looking at the young woman with him.

When the poor chap relied yes, the performer told him: "Fantastic! So much prettier than the one you were with yesterday."

"DID YOU see," said the chap in the pub, "that Noel Gallagher said he quit Oasis as he couldn't work with his brother?"

"Well," replied his mate, "we knew that three albums ago."

HIGHLIGHT of Glasgow's Aye Write! book festival was Glasgow poet Tom Leonard, who constantly fights for the Glasgow vernacular to be rated as highly as so-called "proper" English.

Musing on his website about the £7 ticket price, which will raise far more than he is being paid, Tom writes: "The rake-off I imagine will be needed to pay for the hotels and sizeable fees of the media celebs who are travelling from England.

"I've no doubt that if I was one of these whom the festival organisers think of as 'recognised in England, and in the English papers', council culture committee members would consider it a significant honour to be allowed to wipe my bum should I go to the toilet."

Sheer poetry Tom.

WE LOVE it when Edinburgh Fringe performers come into contact with real people.

Comedian Jeffrey Solomon performed Mother/Son, in which he played two characters based loosely on himself and his mother, so was carrying a handbag he uses as a prop when he popped into a nearby bar. Trying to leave, he was stopped by a steward who asked why he had a woman's handbag – quite right, he could have just nicked it.

He explained he used it in his show.

"Do you have any proof you are a performer?" asked the steward.

Jeffrey told him even more about the show, only to be asked again: "Have you got any proof you are a performer?"

Ego severely bruised, Jeffrey had to stand there as the steward went through the handbag checking up on what he clearly believed was a far-fetched story.

APPEARING at the Edinburgh Fringe was Irish comedian Peadar de Burca whose show *What Men Want* reveals men's insecurities.

Says Peadar: "I was once amongst the audience, and asked the question, 'If a man speaks deep in a forest and there is no woman there to hear him, is he still wrong?' when a woman stood up, said, 'Yes,' and punched me in the mouth, drawing blood.

"Her friends got her out as she roared, 'I'll kill him!'

"I was all set to make a quip about how pissed off her psychiatrist was going to be, when the fire alarm went off and in runs yer one through the doors, shouting, 'Who's laughing now?'"

SCOTS violinist Nicola Benedetti tells us about performing at a Classic FM concert in Manchester. When she collected her thoughts before a slow, considered piece, the audience went quiet, waiting politely for her to start playing.

Except for one eager Glaswegian who, breaking the silence, screamed out: "Come on, Nikki, show us what you can do."

BARRIE CRAWFORD tells us that health and safety has become involved in the festive song 'Jingle Bells' and the verse: 'Dashing through the snow, On a one-horse open sleigh, O'er the fields we go, Laughing all the way.'

An H&S official writes: "A risk assessment must be submitted before an open sleigh is considered safe for members of the public. It must also consider whether it is appropriate to use only one horse, particularly if passengers are of larger proportions.

"Please note, permission is required from landowners before entering their fields. To avoid offending those not participating in celebrations, we would request that laughter is not loud enough to be considered a noise nuisance."

# 16
## Beer Sledges

**Glasgow is the shopping capital of Britain outside London. And you can't go shopping without creating a laugh or two.**

A READER shopping in a Greenock supermarket, with only a few items, was stuck behind a woman at the checkout with a large pile of groceries. His mood wasn't helped when the woman suddenly announced: "Oh, I've forgotten something!" and dashed back up the aisles.

He was surprised, though, when she returned a few minutes later pushing a young child in a buggy.

LUCY MACK was in the Argyle Street branch of bookseller Waterstone's when the heavens opened outside, and folk were running in all directions to get shelter from the rain. Two ned-like chaps ran into Waterstone's, stopped in their tracks, looked around, and one declared: "Aw, naw, it's a bluidy bookshop," before both ran back out into the rain.

OUR STORY about neds sheltering from rain reminds a Bishop-briggs reader of being in Fraser's store in Glasgow when a potential customer asked an assistant: "Hey, bud, are these jackets waterproof?"

When the assistant confirmed that they were, the customer persisted: "Even if it's pishin' doon?"

Without batting an eyelid, the assistant replied: "Yes, even in heavy rain."

COLIN McNICOLL from Braco was waiting patiently in a baker's shop where a mother and daughter were spending ages deciding which cake they would buy as a treat to themselves. After much ooohing and aaahing at the collection through the glass, they finally left with a coffee and walnut cake. At that the assistant said to her colleague: "Dear God, I chose my house quicker than that."

A READER claimed he went in to PC World and asked if they could recommend a hard drive.

"Through Larkhall in a green car," the assistant replied.

WE ALWAYS assumed that an author signing his book added to its value to readers. Not so in Glasgow's Waterstone's in Sauchiehall Street, where a reader watched an elderly woman pick up a signed novel, only for her friend to tell her: "Don't get that one – someone's written oan it."

A READER tells us he was in the local butcher's when the customer in front of him was getting annoyed at her little daughter whispering something she couldn't make out.

The woman snapped at the girl: "Didn't I tell you not to whisper?"

At that, the girl's voice could be heard around the shop as she loudly asked: "Mummy, why has that lady got a moustache?"

THE NEWS story about attempts to protect the name Lorne Sausage reminds reader Isobel MacDonald of being in her local butcher's when an old fella asked the owner if he put rusk in his square sausage.

The butcher replied of course, as that's what binds it together.

"Aye," said the worthy, "there was that much rusk in it, I didn't know whether to grill it or put milk on it."

"HE MUST be great at his job," said the young lad staring in the window of a key cutting shop in Glasgow. "Look at all the trophies he's got."

READER Elizabeth Cockburn praises the entrepreneurial skill of an Irvine shopkeeper who had plastic sledges for sale in his window in June. Next to them was a card stating "Beer Sledges for T in the Park".

AN AYSHIRE reader returning to Scotland on a Ryanair flight asked for a can of Coke, which the stewardess said was 80p. As the cans were tiny, he asked for two, and was surprised that she then pulled out a calculator and started tapping away.

"I don't know what surprised me most," he tells us. "That or her answer, 'That will be £1.40, sir'."

THE ARITHMETICALLY-CHALLENGED stewardess who took out a calculator to work out the cost of two cans of Coke reminds David Macleod in Lenzie of when he asked in a shop for ten stamps. He was told: "We only sell them in books of six or four."

GLASWEGIANS have been reminiscing about the grocery chain Henry Healy's, which has shut. As a lady called Maggie recalls on the website *Glasgow Guide*: "My job as a junior was to pick up the bits of bacon that had fallen on the floor, put them on a tray, rinse them under cold water to remove the sawdust and make sure they were strategically placed between the nice slices so that they wouldn't be noticed, but would make up the weight.

"My family were always warned not to buy butter or bacon first thing in the morning.

"I loved every minute in that shop."

JAC McDIARMID, who once ran a greetings card shop in Port Glasgow, tells us sympathy cards were among the best sellers. She once heard a customer, who was buying a sympathy card and a get-well card, being asked by an acquaintance in the queue who it was that "wasnae well" and "who's deid".

The card buyer explained who was ill, then added that the sympathy card was "just in case".

A READER swears that he was in a branch of Tesco when a little old woman standing at the information desk waiting for a member of staff to come along looked at the slogan "Every little helps" above it and told him: "They should drop the first and last letters."

A READER was in the Edinburgh florist shop Flower this week when a chap came in to order a large bouquet. The florist wrote down the message he wanted on the card, then, thinking of a final flourish to add, asked: "Will you want kisses?"

"I'll be expecting a lot more than that!" the chap replied.

A PARTICK reader spotted in his supermarket that toilet rolls were on offer at twelve for the price of nine. In addition, there was a three-for-two offer on the packs, so he picked up six of the large packs and headed to the check-out.

As the girl scanned the huge pile of rolls she told him: "I'm surprised you risked coming to the shops."

A READER felt for the middle-aged father shopping in Glasgow's HMV store with his teenage daughter. She interrupted his story about going to a Rod Stewart concert in his youth, so he asked: "Have I told you this before?"

"So many times," his daughter replied, "I can't believe you're not in a nursing home."

A READER in Glasgow watched a young lad get a red face in a coffee shop when, ordering a coffee, he asked the server: "How big are your cups?"

"That's a bit personal," she replied.

HAMILTON t-shirt printers Dynamic Grafix had a customer who wanted a shirt printed for his wife who had recently been to New York with friends on a shopping trip, and a hefty credit-card bill had ensued.

He asked for a shirt with the usual "I love NY" on the front, and on the back "Veni, Vidi, Visa" roughly translated as "I came, I saw, I spent".

A READER spots a father doing the shopping in Morrisons with two young children, and his hesitant approach to where he was going suggested he didn't do the shopping often.

The chap picked up a packet and read from the back: "All natural ingredients."

He put it back and told the kids: "You would just have told me it didn't taste right."

READER Cathy Macdonald was in a Largs butcher's which is famous for its range of steak pies. A wee wummin in front couldn't decide on what size of steak pie she wanted. The butcher, trying to help, asked how many it was to feed. Without hesitation, she replied: "Two and a dug."

AFTER the Tesco store in Cardiff banned shoppers in pyjamas, reader Dougie Lyden tells us of being in a Partick sandwich shop when

a girl in regulation pyjamas and fake Ugg boots asked for a "tuna melt panini withoot cheese".

The serving lady replied: "So you're wantin' a tuna toastie then, hen?"

After a little thought, the customer said: "Naw, that sounds boggin'. Gies two Scotch pies."

"So nearly a continental lunch experience . . . yet so far," says Dougie.


A READER buying *The Herald* overheard a couple who were peering at the small ads in the newsagent's window, with the female declaring: "There's a three-piece suite here at a good price – in the right colour, too."

The chap, clearly not keen on the idea, came up with the inspired reply: "Did your parents not warn you not to take suites from strangers?"


THE BATTLE OF THE BOYNE was fought in Ireland in 1690 between the Protestant Prince William and the Catholic King James. Carfin, near Motherwell, was settled by mainly Irish Catholics, proud of their roots to this day.

We only mention these two facts as Frank the manager of the Mandarin Restaurant in Motherwell made a home delivery to a Carfin resident who naturally asked how much. Frank read the label and told him: "Sixteen ninety."

"Not in Carfin it's not," the chap replied.

"Will we say £17 then?" asked Frank.

"Deal," replied his customer.

TALKING of Lanarkshire, a reader was in his local off-licence there when a young chap picked up a bottle of fortified wine, which accidentally dropped to the floor and smashed. The shop owner called over: "You'll have to pay for that."

Our reader thought the young chap's reply was inspired. "I'm not 18," he stated.


A READER in the changing rooms of a large Glasgow store watched as a young girl came out to show her mum the clothes she had been trying on. The mother, not overly impressed by the colour black in both her skirt and top, asked: "Are you planning on going to a funeral?"

Undeterred, the daughter replied: "Well, there are a lot of auld yins in our family."


A READER overhears a tired shopper near the Donald Dewar statue in Glasgow's Buchanan Street arrange with his wife for them to go their separate ways and link up later. His parting shot to his good lady was: "I'll meet you outside Pappy Are Us in half an hour."

We guess he was dogging school the day his history class was discussing the ancient Egyptian art of paper-making.


AS ROBERT ALEXANDER'S butchers in Port Glasgow has won an award for the best beef links in the west of Scotland, we forgive owner Drew McKenzie for telling us: "The links were made from a recipe used by my late grandfather, Bob Alexander, whose shop sign said, 'Robert Alexander, Quality Butcher. Noted for our sausages.'

"A woman asked him one day, 'Bob, what are your sausages noted for?'

"'Well', he says, 'if they wernae noted, the meat wid come oot the ends.'"

Let's hope Drew's sausages are never as old as that.

# 17
# A Last Farewell

**We say goodbye to some good friends.**

RADIO LUXEMBOURG DJ from the 1970s and 1980s, Dave Christian, who died, was remembered by Luxembourg reader Alun Hotchkiss. Alan recalls the time Dave, who had an encyclopaedic knowledge of music, declared in a pub that he would bet anyone a pint that if they came up with a name, he could think of a song with the name in it. Someone tried to fox him with an obscure name, but Dave screwed his face up in intense concentration then announced: "Got it!" and sang: "Happy Birthday to you, happy birthday to you ..."

A FUNERAL director tells us he thought he had heard all the unusual music requests for services until he attended a burial recently where mod band The Jam's 'Going Underground' blared out from the speakers.

CREMATIONS, continued. George Ferguson in Castlecary tells us of a recent service which was interrupted by a mobile phone ringing among the mourners. "What made matters worse," says George, "was the ring tone was 'Don'tcha wish your girlfriend was hot like me?'"

FORMER rugby internationalist Kenny Logan recalled the late, great commentator Bill McLaren giving him a Hawick Ball sweet before an international game and telling him it would make him run faster.

Kenny joked with him that he had given Hawick Balls to so many players that he wouldn't be any faster than the rest of them.

"Aye," replied Bill, "but I never gave any to the English."

THE DEATH of Chic Murray's wife and fellow performer Maidie reminds Matt Vallance of when there was a fire in the Edinburgh hotel that Chic and Maidie owned and managed. Chic told a news-paper reporting on it: "I can honestly say, in all the years we've been married, it's the first time I've ever seen the wife take a bucket."

THE DEATH of Sir Ludovic Kennedy reminds Roger Mullin in Kirkcaldy of how elegantly Ludo could deliver a put-down, even of former American presidents.

Sir Ludovic was addressing a political meeting in Maybole Town Hall during the seventies when a member of the audience asked if he had come all the way from London for the meeting, recalls Roger.

"Certainly not," replied Ludo. "I live in Scotland and come from a long line of Scottish Kennedys."

He then added: "Those who couldn't make it here in Scotland

emigrated to Ireland, and those who couldn't make it there moved to Massachusetts."

HARRY CONROY, the former *Daily Record* man and National Union of Journalists general secretary who has died, had numerous run-ins with megalomaniac publisher Robert Maxwell. Harry once recalled that Maxwell one Christmas sent the staff a royal family souvenir book, each containing a commemorative sovereign. Management put a security guard on the 1,000 books, fearing theft. They needn't have bothered. When distributed, it was discovered Maxwell had already removed all the sovereigns.

GLASGOW'S Old Fruitmarket was packed for Billfest – a tribute night for the late trade union leader Bill Speirs. His old pal, actor Elaine C Smith, recalled when she was appearing in Calendar Girls in London, a lawyer friend in Glasgow would send her snippets to remind her of the dear green place.

She included the court case of a woman attacked by an ex-boyfriend. The victim was giving evidence, and the fiscal, to show the woman seldom went out, asked her: "So this was a rare night out?"

"Hardly a rare night out. I got stabbed," the woman replied.

ONE OF Bill's old trade union colleagues attending Billfest sported a lapel badge, which proclaimed: "Guy Fawkes. The only man to go to parliament and not claim expenses."

ONE WAY of trying to make money is to register domain names on the internet in the hope that they will become valuable in the future. Somehow we are equally appalled yet admiring of the fact that according to domain name registry 123-reg, the day after singer Michael Jackson died, someone registered the site thejacksonfour.co . . .

SAD TO see the death of broadcaster Steve Hamilton, the first DJ heard on Radio Forth, and off screen *Wheel of Fortune* announcer. Steve, who held masterclasses for fledgling broadcasters, once told his pupils that even the most skilled public speaker can be lost for words – and gave the example of hosting a Radio Forth show from a local hospital where he cheerily asked a patient: "Back on your feet again soon?"

"No, I've just had my legs amputated," the patient replied.

SOCIAL worker turned crime writer Reg McKay always had a twinkle in his eye, no matter with whom he was dealing.

Reg once told us about being pinned down in Rogano by a London film producer who desperately wanted to talk about Glasgow crime lords. Just then, the late, lamented, imposing Glasgow lawyer Martin Smith walked in, and Reg bought him a drink.

The excitable Londoner asked Reg: "He must be a major gangster, eh?"

Not wishing to lie, but willing to string him along, Reg replied: "Well, put it this way: I bought him a drink."

The producer was so impressed he sent across an additional large one to Martin, while telling Reg: "Well, you have to show your respect to these blokes, don't you?"

# 18
# Politically Incorrect

**Even politics can make us smile occasionally.**

HEADLINE on the BBC website "David Cameron says 'I will turn UK around.'" Or, as one *Herald* reader commented: "That's great! I've always wanted Scotland to be nearer France."

PRIME MINISTER David Cameron, on a visit to Scotland during the election, said he had written to then Prime Minister Gordon Brown to ask if he had any objections to him touring his Kirkcaldy constituency and talking to the voters.

Brown, said Cameron, had merely replied with a curt, "No, you can't."

"Mind you," added the Tory leader, "it was the strangest spelling of 'can't' that I'd seen."

AN ASSISTANT to a Scottish MP tells us he was in a bar very close to the Houses of Parliament at closing time one night recently when the barman, trying to cajole imbibers to drink up, shouted out: "Come on. Have you no second homes to go to?"

NEWS from Diary chum Tom Harris, the Glasgow Labour MP, back at Westminster after the election, who bumped into Yorkshire Tory MP Bob Goodwill.

Says Tom: "Bob suggested he was considering growing a Hitler moustache and wearing round, horn-rimmed glasses.

"Intrigued by this unexpected revelation, we inquired further. He explained, 'Because then it will make defacing my posters utterly pointless.'"

FORMER Scottish Secretary Jim Murphy was at the Midlothian Innovation Centre in Roslin to open a bio-mass centre at Stobo House, named after veteran agriculturist James Stobo. A delighted Mr Stobo, who was at the event, said he was very touched by the honour of having the building carrying his name, and would regard Stobo House as his second home.

"You should not," explained Murphy, "mention the words 'second home' in front of MPs."

"DID YOU hear that they wanted to name a locomotive after Gordon Brown?" said the loudmouth in a London pub. "But after the expenses scandal they didn't want to spend a lot of money."

He added: "So someone came up with the idea of going to the National Railway Museum and chiselling the 'F' off of the *Flying Scotsman.*

"Sorted."

A READER is confused about the British National Party's website calling the sending home of al Megrahi from a Scottish jail as "treason". He tells us: "Yet in almost every other page of their site, they are demanding that foreigners should be sent home. How strange."

A READER spots the BBC news headline: "Osborne to spell out planned cuts," and ponders: "Fair enough, George, but once you've finished practising your spelling, do you think you could do something about the economy?"

THE ELECTION campaign reminds Gregor Young of many years ago working in Errol on election day when a rich retired couple drove down to the polling station in their Bentley with blue ribbons for the Tories attached to their car. The couple employed a chauffeur, so the sight of the rich chap's wife driving the Bentley was a rare one. When asked why, they told locals: "We gave him the day off – as we knew he would only vote Labour if he drove us down."

RICHARD GAULT recalls Maggie Thatcher visiting Oban while electioneering and arriving by helicopter. As she descended, she noticed one of the waiting police officers had a camera, so she paused at the door and said: "Well, what are you waiting for?"

The embarrassed officer, a plane spotter, had to tell her he was waiting for her to move as he wanted to get a picture of the helicopter.

COST conscious Glasgow councillors debated whether there should be a civic dinner to mark comedian Billy Connolly being given the Freedom of the City. Council leader Gordon Matheson won everyone over by declaring: "Of course we'll give him his tea – it's not Edinburgh he's getting the Freedom of the City from."

FORMER Celtic star Frank McAvennie tells us of when he met Margaret Thatcher in the dressing room before the 1988 Scottish Cup final. Normally the presentation is done on the pitch, but some fans were shouting unkind words about the Prime Minister, so it was switched.

Frank wound up captain Roy Aitken by saying he was going to chat to Mrs Thatcher, and, when he was introduced, Frank raised her gloved hand, kissed it and said: "I'd just like to thank you very much."

As she looked puzzled, he added: "As a high earner, for cutting the top rate of income tax."

When she moved on, and Aitken glowered at him, Frank told him: "Blondes and me – a wonderful combination."

"DID YOU see that Barack Obama is sending an extra 30,000 troops to Afghanistan?" declared the chap in the pub the other night. "Brilliant! Give the man a Nobel peace prize."

WE FEEL sorry for Liz Cameron, Glasgow's former Lord Provost, being berated by striking museum staff over the number of foreign trips she has undertaken on official business. "So we're supposed to tighten our belts," one of the strikers told us, "when the only belt-tightening Liz has been doing is her aircraft seatbelt."

# 19
## It's Only a Flea Bite

**They say laughter is the best medicine. But I would always insist on some antibiotics as well, just to be on the safe side.**

A READER tells us he was attending a fracture clinic where he got into conversation with a chap having his leg, which was in a stookie, checked. The man said he was a former window cleaner. Our reader asked him when he'd given up the job, which allowed the chap to give his prepared answer: "Halfway doon."

READER Elaine Morgan in Ottawa, Canada, tells us: "I'm being sent to see a lung specialist named Dr Kronick. "I was really hoping to see his colleague, Dr Itllpassinafewdays."

OUR STORY of the chap told by his doc to get breathless more often, so he took up smoking, reminds Dennis Kelly of the yarn about the chap who booked into a hotel and asked the receptionist for a wake-up call.

"You're overweight, losing you hair and need to start drinking less," she replied.

"I'VE JUST been to the doc's and diagnosed with low blood pressure," said the chap in the pub. "So I told him I'd just bought a self-assembly wardrobe from Ikea. That should fix it."

A SOUTH SIDE reader attending a Weight-Watchers' meeting heard the organiser taking the money, who wanted to apologise to everyone waiting, tell the woman at the front of the queue: "Sorry for your wait."

However, the customer merely replied: "It's my own fault – I need willpower."

"I WENT to the doc's," said the chap in the pub the other night, "with a terrible pain in my foot. The first thing he said to me was, 'Gout.'

"But I told him, 'Hang on, I've just got here.'"

A NURSE who carries out drug tests on potential staff being hired by an American company in Scotland felt one chap didn't help his employment prospects when he replied: "Drug tests? Aye, line them up. I'll gie anything a shot."

A FEMALE gym-attender tells us: "Note to blokes at the gym: try stepping away from staring at the full-length mirror and actually lift some weights.

"Just a thought."

A CUMBERNAULD reader visiting his wife in Airdrie's Monklands Hospital was asked by the physiotherapist if he was the patient's partner. When he jokingly replied that the phrase made him sound like a cowboy from a Hopalong Cassidy film, the physio explained that he had been working at the hospital for three days and he was the first husband he had met.

But that's Lanarkshire for you, someone may or may not say.

A BIT HARSH surely, thought the reader, who saw a young person wearing a t-shirt on which the slogan read: "Bulimia: twice the taste but none of the calories."

OUR MENTION of t-shirt slogans reminds Campbell Read of seeing a mum with baby twins. The baby girl was dressed in a pink shirt with the slogan: "All mummy wanted was a cuddle."

A DOCTOR tells us of concerns about medical record transcription being outsourced to cheaper companies abroad, and the possibility of mistakes creeping in. He says that one doctor had reported on a patient's vein inflammation as "phlebitis, left leg". The report came back typed up as "flea bite his left leg".

A BEARSDEN woman told her pals she and her husband had been trying for some time to have a baby.

"Wear gold jewellery and a tracksuit," said her pal.

"How will that help?" she asked.

"Have you ever seen a young woman with gold jewellery and a tracksuit who wasn't pushing a buggy?"

A GLASGOW reader tells us about temporarily losing her voice, but as she had a hairdresser's appointment she went along with a note explaining she was unable to chat. Miraculously, she was back out in the street in fifteen minutes. She's now wondering if she should do that again if she is ever pressed for time.

SOME opposition politicians expressed doubts over Lockerbie bomber Abdelbaset Ali Mohmed al-Megrahi's illness because he lived longer than the forecasted three months. But as a bar-room philosopher opined: "The suggestion that he had only three months to live was made when he was in Greenock . . ."

A BEARSDEN reader, trying to keep fit after the New Year, went for a run that ended with the short, steep hill up to the reservoir at Milngavie. He reached the top and was bending over with his hands on his knees, catching his breath, when an old dear out for a stroll with her pal asked: "Would you like to borrow my inhaler?"

A READER hears an old fella in the bar complain that he plucked up the courage to ask his doctor for a course of Viagra, but the doc had turned him down. When his pal asked why, the chap replied: "He said it would be as much use as putting a new flagpole on a condemned building."

READER Jimmy Graham, visiting a relative at the Victoria Infirmary, carefully used the disinfectant hand gel before entering the ward. Minutes later, a track-suited chap in his forties walked straight in with a fish supper, shared it with the woman he was visiting, then carefully wiped his hands on the bed covers.

Perhaps he just read the bit about cleaning your hands.

[ 157 ]

THE H1N1 swine flu vaccine should not be taken if you are allergic to eggs as the vaccine is produced in chicken eggs and thus contains traces of egg protein.

This fact was not known to the elderly lady overheard on a Glasgow bus this week who told her pal it was odd that her doc, giving the swine flu jab, asked if she was allergic to eggs.

"I mean," she went on, "what's that to do with pigs? They don't have eggs."

Her pal pondered this conundrum for a few moments before coming up with the solution: "Ah, but you eat bacon with eggs. That must be the connection."

And, thus, with the medical problem solved, the conversation turned to the weather.

BEFORE a crucial Old Firm game at Ibrox, we resurrect the old gag about the two Celtic fans desperate to see their team at Ibrox, but who could only get tickets among the Rangers fans.

Neither wore his Celtic scarf in order to blend in, but when Celtic scored one of them couldn't stop jumping up and cheering. He awoke in a hospital ward where his unharmed pal had arrived with grapes.

"How come they didn't touch you?" asked the fan in the hospital bed.

"Well, I was the first to get steamed into you," his pal replied.

# 10
## Kid's Play

WE HEAR about a father, putting on a fresh shirt, and grumbling at his two angelic sons sitting on the sofa: "Other weans make their mothers too tired to want to go out – but not you two."

WE WON'T name and shame the Scottish dad who, when his six-year-old son worried about the Tooth Fairy not coming as his tooth had fallen out in the playground and he couldn't find it, suggested he draw a picture of the tooth instead and put it under his pillow. That night, dad crept up, removed the drawing – and replaced it with a drawing of a pound.

JOE HUGHES recalled living in Dunfermline where a large open space was used for football by local kids who damaged the fences of neighbouring gardens. So complaints were made to the council. Eventually, two poles with signs stating "No football" were erected at either end of the open space. Overnight, one of the signs was transplanted from one end and installed at the other to make a perfect set of goalposts with the other sign.

A FATHER tells us his young son wanted to see a film called *Up You*. He thought that rather a demotic phrase for a wholesome film and checked *The Herald* film guide, relieved to learn it was in fact *Up* (U).

WE HEAR a teenager telling his pals that by coincidence his Higher grades were the same as his favourite band: ACDC. He added that he now wished he'd been an ABBA fan instead.

A GIFFNOCK mother came back from Christmas shopping defeated at being unable to find a shop that had not sold out of this year's "must have" gift for little girls: Go Go Hamsters – little motorised hamsters made in China.

Trying to be sympathetic, her husband told her: "If only there was an alternative – something hamster-like that moved about. We could even put it in a ball to run around the front room, and at night it could sleep in a cage.

"If only . . ."

A MOTHER tells us she got "a bit of a reddy" when she took her young children to a family reunion in a restaurant and ordered a bottle of wine for the company. When the waiter brought the bottle and poured a little into her glass to taste, the moment was spoiled by her nine-year-old loudly remarking: "Mummy usually has a lot more than that."

WE WERE discussing the age-old problem of how to keep children amused with prominent Glasgow lawyer Austin Lafferty, who told us that his wife was having a cup of tea in the vast Silverburn shopping centre when a big Glasgow family commandeered the next table.

Said Austin: "The children were obstreperous, especially one young girl who was shouting the odds and running around to everyone's annoyance.

"Eventually her mother, hard-pressed with a babe in arms also squalling, had a brainwave, and asked the wee girl, 'Haw, Abigail, want tae come and watch me wipe yer sister's arse?'"

THERE is a rise, of course, in the use of more exotic names for children. Angela Ross tells us she was in a shoe shop where a little lad was hiding from his mum behind the racks. Eventually the exasperated mother came out with the virtually Shakespearean bellow: "Romeo! Romeo! Where ur ye Romeo?"

A WHALE swimming in the River Clyde at Glasgow drew curious crowds to the riverbank. A Radio Scotland reporter interviewing the crowds recorded an excitable child shouting: "Err it's there." The moment was then spoiled by the child's mother adding: "Naw, ratza duck."

A READER on the train from Edinburgh to Inverness watched as a little boy with his mum pointed to a house in the middle of a field with no other buildings around, and asked who lived there.

"Maybe a hermit," replied his mum.

Then a thought occurred to her. "Do you know what a hermit is?" she asked the little one.

"Yes," the lad confidently replied. "A frog."


READER David Dundas hears a wee lad at the shops ask his mum: "Do you think we could afford this?"

"Probably," his mother replied, "but we would need to give something up."

"What's that, mum?" asked the boy.

"Food – for a week," she told him.


A READER suppressed a smile as he passed an exasperated mother in a Glasgow shop the other day who slapped her daughter across the backside and scolded: "Don't you ever do that again!"

The youngster merely stood her ground and replied: "Well, are you happy with yourself?"


A BEARSDEN reader who took her children to a fete was watching a young chap making balloon animals when her young daughter asked him: "What are you making?"

With an exaggerated sigh, he replied: "Minimum wage."


WENDY HUNTER was at a parents' orientation event at the University of California, Santa Barbara, when a lecturer answered a question about how you ensure your kid keeps in touch once he's gone to uni.

He told parents: "Send them a card saying how you realise that they must be studying really hard and attending so many classes, that you have put a cheque in the card, and tell them to cash it, and go out and have some fun for a change."

When the parent asked how this would solve the problem, he replied: "Don't put the cheque in and see how quickly he'll phone you."

"I WAS listening to music when I realised I needed to pass wind," we hear a teenager tell his pals. In fact, he might not have said "pass wind".

"I waited until a really loud bit of the music, so that folk wouldn't hear me," he continued.

"It was only afterwards that it dawned on me that I was listening to the music on my iPod, so that didn't really work."

THE CLOSURE of the Queen Mum's maternity hospital in Glasgow reminds a reader of being in the waiting room there when a father came through from where his wife was expecting a child.

He was surrounded by a gaggle of excitable relatives including one young girl who shouted: "Well? Am I an aunty or an uncle?"

A READER in a branch of fast-food supplier McDonald's heard a woman with a young son ask if they did Miserable Meals. When the staff member asked if she meant a Happy Meal, the woman replied: "Well, I'd get him a Happy Meal, but he's been a miserable wee sod all day."

OUR STORY about mother-of-two actress Ruthie Henshall putting "What's that?" under 'Recreation' in *Who's Who*, reminds Bob Byiers of his sister-in-law being interviewed by a researcher.

Says Bob: "With two young children scrambling for attention around her feet, when asked, 'What do you do in your spare time?' she answered, 'I go to the toilet!'"

AND NOVELIST Meg Henderson says that when the last of her three children went to school, she celebrated, she tells us, "the end of years of being trailed everywhere by multiple footsteps, by going to the loo and leaving the door wide open."

A BEARSDEN reader who took his family for a run was a bit lost for words when they came to a warning sign with an exclamation mark in the middle, and below it "Hidden Dip". His young daughter asked: "Why did they hide it?"

A PAISLEY reader tells us she was fed up with her son not keeping his promise to feed his goldfish and, as she once again fed it, she shouted at him: "How many times would that poor fish have died if it wasn't for me?"

She had to admit that her son's reply of, "Just the once," was, of course, accurate.

# 21
# Worse Than Taxi Drivers

A READER travelling by train on the Highland line tells us there was much debate on board about how tricky the toilets are if you press the wrong button – either trapping folk inside or, worse, suddenly opening at an inopportune moment. At that, one local told fellow travellers: "That's why we call them the kami-khazis."

A GLASGOW woman tells us her car wouldn't start, but when she phoned her breakdown cover provider she was told she wasn't covered for problems when the car was in her driveway – only when it was out on the road. "What if I pushed it out on to the road?" she asked.

   "Well," replied the call centre chap, "we're only responsible for getting you home – so we'd push it back."

CELIA STEVENSON was travelling on a late-night train from Edinburgh to Glasgow when she overheard a reveller tell his pal that a mutual friend had a new girlfriend who was "completely uninhabited". Perhaps she's from St Kilda.

BRUCE SKIVINGTON was on a train to Inverness that was jam-packed with mainly beer-and-tent carrying music fans heading to the Rock Ness Festival. At Perth, an old fella struggled on with bags and, incongruously, a broom. The conductor looked at the broom, and the old chap told him: "Look, if we break down, the wife can use this to go for help."

A GLASGOW taxi driver tells us a colleague picked up a passenger late at night from one of the city's casinos. When the driver asked where to, the passenger, in an unfunny attempt to portray that he had lost a lot of money that night, replied: "Erskine Bridge."

The driver, not cracking a light, replied: "Cash up front."

A HYNDLAND reader on business in America heard the flight attendant tell passengers to turn their cell phones to airplane mode. The attendant then added: "If you are unsure how to do this, ask a nearby child for assistance."

BUS COMPANY Stagecoach offered to replace the closure-threatened Renfrew Ferry with an amphibious bus called the Amfibus. Reader Ian Maclean tells us Derek Mackay, leader of Renfrewshire Council, backed the idea, but wanted it renamed the AmfiRenfrewbus.

A BUSINESSMAN in the back of a Glasgow taxi watched as a bus cut in front of the cab, making the driver brake sharply. "See bus drivers," exclaimed his driver. "They're worse than taxi drivers."

THE COST of car insurance was being discussed by a few chaps at an Ayrshire golf club when the philosopher further up the bar opined: "Car insurance is a bit like wearing a hospital gown – you're never actually covered as much as you think you are."

A COMMUTER on a train into Glasgow Central Station heard two young chaps in tracksuits becoming increasingly agitated about the train stopping just a few hundred yards short of the station. "We're gonny be late!" one of them snapped. "What a rubbish service!"

After they moaned a bit longer, the second one added: "Glad ah didnae buy a ticket."

READER Marion Daly, from Houston, was in Glasgow Airport when there was a last call for a British Midland flight to Heathrow, and they were urging Messrs Whyte, McKay and Bell to go to the plane. "They'll be in the bar," Marion thought to herself.

A GLASGOW reader tells us his son Jack got a job as a member of an airline's cabin crew. When he returned home after his first few weeks in the job, he explained that the only downside was the number of passengers who actually thought it was funny, when they saw his name tag, to say "Hi Jack" to him when they boarded the plane.

AN EDINBURGH chap travelling by train found a fellow commuter sitting in his reserved seat, and rather than pointing this out to the chap, he decided instead to tell the guard, or whatever they are called these days, in the way that some folk from Edinburgh do.

The guard, possibly having a hectic day, and feeling that the chap should sort it out himself, gave him the advice: "Just go back and tell him to **** off."

We suspect the guard had been absent on the staff training day covering courtesy to passengers.

WE OVERHEAR a young chap in Byres Road pointing out an RAC van stuck in traffic to his pal, and declaring: "Do you see how depressed the driver in that van looks?"

When his pal looked puzzled, it of course allowed him to add: "I think he's heading for a breakdown."

A READER on holiday in London was on the Jubilee Underground line when the driver came on to announce over the public address system: "This train will terminate at West Ham – like many footballers' careers."

A BEARSDEN reader tells us he was getting a taxi home, and was chatting to the driver who was saying he enjoyed working for himself and being his own boss. The driver has just finished telling him: "No one tells me what to do," when our reader had to say: "Stop here."

READER Willie Sharp tells us: "With the introduction of full body X-ray scans, this is another opportunity for Ryanair to increase its profits. It will now be able to charge each passenger £10 for the privilege of being scanned, £15 for a copy of the X-ray, and £35 for a copy of someone else's."

# 22
# CSI Kilwinning

WE HEAR the folk in Airdrie are in a state of shock over the news that guns used in a gangland killing were found dumped behind a library in neighbouring Coatbridge. They had no idea that Coatbridge had a library.

READER Alun Hotchkiss tells us he was in a restaurant when the maitre d' asked a couple if they had reservations, and the chap replied: "Yes, but we're hungry so we'll eat here anyway."

"WHY DO folk who run television companies," asked the philosopher in the golf club the other day, "assume that people who are deaf are also insomniacs."

ON ASH WEDNESDAY, it seemed in these irreligious days, that fewer people are aware of Catholics having ash on their foreheads to remind us that we return to ash and dust.

One churchgoer returning to her office was asked by a colleague what the mark was on her forehead.

She replied it was ashes, and her colleague, not the brightest admittedly, asked who's funeral had she been at.

A READER claims he went to visit his student son in Dundee and, reaching the student flats, wasn't sure if he was pressing the right buzzer, so he asked the person who answered: "Does Davey live here?"

He was concerned about the reply of: "Aye. Just leave him there and we'll collect him later."

DONALD SHIELDS spots that someone had scrawled "Bolloks" in the toilets at North Glasgow College. Above it someone had written

the letter "C" with an arrow pointing to its proper location, and added beside it in brackets: "I'll keep you right, son."

NATALIE O'DONNELL tells us she heard a chap in Glasgow on the phone to a call centre in India who he was having difficulty being understood. Eventually the operative in India asked the caller to spell his name phonetically, and Natalie wonders how much understanding there was when the chap started with: "M...for Monster Munch."

THE RAF's retiring of the Nimrod aircraft at RAF Kinloss reminds Hugh Campbell of the local in Easter Ross with the nickname Nimrod – as he was always on the lookout for a sub.

THE LATEST keeping up with the Joneses trend. A reader claims his neighbour painted a large blue rectangle in his back garden so that people looking at the area on Google Earth would think he had a swimming pool.

READER Frank Eardley overheard a chap discussing a wedding he attended, and when asked what the bride's family were like, the chap replied: "I wouldn't say they were rough, but when they were being photographed they automatically held out their hands expecting to be fingerprinted as well."

AN EDINBURGH reader swears that a chap having coffee in Starbucks told the business acquaintance with him: "I'm such an idiot. I forgot my sister's birthday last week."

His friend tried to reassure him that it not an uncommon slip-up, but the chap then added: "But we're twins."

A YOUNG chap in Glasgow's Byres Road was spotted pointing to an attractive young woman crossing the road and telling his mate: "Is she not the hottest thing ever?"

But his mate merely replied: "You've obviously never bitten straight into a fresh McDonald's apple pie."

READER Bill Arnott was cheered up in his local shopping centre by the sheer daftness of a message on a t-shirt a shopper was wearing. It read: "Jesus is coming," and below, it added: "Everybody look busy."

DAVID MARTIN was in Dundee's Phoenix Bar where a customer on his mobile phone was having difficulty being understood at some call centre he was phoning.

Assuming he had been connected to India, the chap bellowed: "I'm in Dundee, it's one o'clock in the afternoon and it's sunny outside. What time is it where you are, and what's the weather like?"

Says David: "When he came off the phone, he told everyone quite sheepishly, 'The guy said it was one o'clock where he was, too, and that, as usual, it was quite chilly in Aberdeen.'"

AN ARGUMENT involving two girls, overheard in Glasgow's Argyle Street train station, ended with the cutting line: "You must get so exhausted putting make-up on two faces each morning. If you're gonna be two-faced at least make one of them pretty!"

SCOTTISH TELEVISION making cheap and cheerful local programmes, rather than paying for expensive network productions, leads to the claim that STV considered making CSI Kilwinning.

However, the programme idea was abandoned as the Kilwinning cases could not be solved by forensics as there were no dental records, and everyone had the same DNA.

Or so we are told.

A READER swears to us that he was in a Glasgow fish and chip shop late on a Friday when a drunk weaved in and asked for a fish supper. The helpful server told him that the fish wouldn't be long.

"Well, it better be fat then," replied the drunk.

JANET WHITE tells us of a conversation in a chip shop one evening where a customer asked for three buttered rolls.

"I've no' got any," the member of staff replied.

"That's rubbish!" said the exasperated customer.

"Aye, well," said the woman serving, "they're called morning rolls for a reason."

READER David McNeill of Lanark read a gadget catalogue, which offered a pillow to use on planes. The advertisement described it as "designed by a pilot unable to sleep on long journeys", and he thinks to himself: "That's not reassuring."

IAN BARNETT was with a colleague who gave a street mendicant a couple of quid and cheerily told him: "Go buy yourself a cup of tea with that."

The beggar replied: "Don't tell me what to do with my money."

A WAITER who worked in an award-winning London restaurant tells us about the first Glaswegian he ever served. When the waiter asked him: "Would you like me to let the wine breathe for a little while before pouring?" the customer replied: "Just pour. I can always give it mouth to mouth resuscitation."

THE GLASGOW information site Glasgow Guide asked Glaswegians for their recollections of the first moon landing forty years ago. One world-weary chap wrote: "I was in the RAF at the time on British-American Phantoms. For us in the West it was a moment of jubilation – we'd beaten the Ruskies to the moon.

"Two months later I was married. Should have gone to the moon, or Russia."

READER Forbes Abercrombie points out: "I did not appreciate how much inflation has affected me until I saw a penny lying in the street and realised I don't pick up anything less than a 10p now."

AH, THE GLASGOW banter. Lynsey Reilly tells us she was on Maryhill Road when she was stopped by a chap who asked: "You goat a len eh a fork?"

When she replied: "No, sorry," he persisted with the explanation: "Ach, it's fir ma Pot Noodle – I'll gerrit back to ye."

Lynsey insisted though: "Nope, definitely don't have one on me."

Thus defeated, he told her: "Cheers anyway, pal," before sloping off.

OUR STORY about the folk you meet on Maryhill Road reminds Michael Gartlan of buying a Chinese takeaway en route to visiting a friend in Maryhill. As he knew the flat he was heading for was near the McDonald's on Maryhill Road, he stopped a passer-by and asked him where the McDonald's branch was.

The chap merely looked down at Michael's Chinese food and replied: "Greedy bastirt," and kept walking.

"I WENT to my mate's birthday party dressed as a spanner, but it turned out it wasn't a fancy dress party after all," said the chap in the pub the other night. "I looked like a right tool," he added.

"I WOULDN'T say he's not that bright," said the chap discussing a mutual friend the other night, "but he's only just discovered that his AM radio still works in the evening."

A HOSPITALITY and catering lecturer tells us he finished a session on nutrition with a class of budding chefs, which he rounded off with a quiz that included a question on listing five food products that can be derived from using milk.

He was hoping for answers such as cheese, yoghurt, cream, butter and so on.

But one bright spark wrote: "Corn Flakes, Rice Krispies, Weetabix, Coco Pops and Cheerios."

A READER overhears two women in a Glasgow coffee shop discussing a friend, and declaring: "I wouldn't say she wasn't the brightest, but she was in the supermarket wanting to buy some scratch, as her new boyfriend was boasting about his mum cooking everything from scratch."

MIXED marriages in Glasgow refer, of course, to a combination of religions rather than races. Susan Howes, now in America, tells us about her marriage in Glasgow where the guests were both Catholic and Church of Scotland.

Says Susan: "The best man commented on the fact that during the wedding ceremony no one knew when to stand up, sit down or kneel.

"He said it was like watching a Mexican wave."

OUR STORY about Glasgow mixed marriages reminds Robert Parkhill in Troon of an American friend in Egypt. The American's parents were originally from Glasgow, so when the pal asked Robert: "Do you know what my father said when I told him I was marrying a Moslem?"

"He said, 'Could be worse, she could be a Catholic,'" replied Robert.

Robert's friend was astounded, and asked: "How could you possibly have known that?"

"Because," said Robert, "the only other thing he would have said was, 'Could be worse, she could be a Protestant.'"